THIS
WAY
UP!

Also by Zig Ziglar

Master Successful Personal Habits

Master Your Goals

Master Your Winning Edge

The Secrets of Successful Selling Habits

THIS WAY UP!

ZIG ZIGLAR

MEDIA

MEDIA

Published 2021 by Gildan Media LLC
aka G&D Media
www.GandDmedia.com

FIRST EDITION 2021

Front cover design by David Rheinhardt of Pyrographx

Design by Meghan Day Healey of Story Horse, LLC

Library of Congress Cataloging-in-Publication Data is available upon request

ISBN: 978-1-7225-0513-4

10   9   8   7   6   5   4   3   2   1

Contents

ONE

Three Kinds of Health

Some years ago, my family and I were eating in a cafeteria in Dallas. It was a new cafeteria, and there was an awful lot of excitement around it. We walked in the front door, and we had to walk down the line this way and then turn around and walk back the other way until we were finally in the serving line to get the food.

At first when we went in, we could not even see the food, but when we got in the second phase of the line, we could look through and see it. I said, "Hey, that looks good. I think I'll try that." Then, a little further on, I said, "Yeah, I want some of that." Then a little further, I'd say, "Yeah, that looks good. I'll try some of that too."

Even if you have a prodigious appetite, you can't eat everything in a cafeteria line. I wanted to pick out the things that appealed to me the most. When I got in line, I was able to immediately determine what I wanted. When we got down to the end of the line, my bill looked like the foreign aid bill of the world, and I reached for my wallet. The lady said, "You don't have to pay until you've eaten the food and you head out the front door."

In a way that's just like life, and in a way it's the exact opposite of life. We can choose exactly what we want life to give us. In the cafeteria line, I was able to choose what I wanted and eat it before I paid for it. But in life, you've got to make the deposit before you can make the withdrawal.

In the game of life, all you need to do is identify what you want, then decide what you are willing to exchange for the things you really want.

What is it that most of us want in life? I'm persuaded beyond any doubt that all of us are interested in health, wealth, and happiness. There are some people who will say, "I don't really want to earn a lot of money." I've always believed that anyone who said that would lie about other things too. Don't misunderstand: I know that many ministers, social workers, and educators did not get into those particular careers because they expected to get rich. I've never seen one yet that would not accept a raise if it were offered.

I'm going to talk about three different kinds of health: *physical health*, *mental health*, and *spiritual health*, because man is physical, mental, and spiritual. If you deal with only one or two of these phases, you're not going to glean all that life has to offer. If you're hurting in one aspect of your life, you're hurting all over.

Let's look at our *physical health* just for a moment. Our physical health is tremendously important. If we take good care of our bodies, they will take us further and faster and enable us to do more with what we've got.

Let me ask you a question: If you had a million-dollar horse, would you invite the neighborhood kids in to feed him? Would you keep him out until two or three in the morning, drinking coffee or something else that might not be good for him? Wouldn't you in fact take care of that million-dollar horse by making certain he got everything that would enable him to perform better? The answer is obviously, yes, you would. Yet we have our million-dollar bodies, which we constantly abuse and never really give a thought about caring for.

Fortunately, in the last few years, many Americans have become aware of this fact, and they're taking better care of their bodies. I've lost some weight. A few years ago, I got on an exercise program. Up until then, my idea of an exercise program would be to fill the tub, take a bath, pull the plug, and fight the current. I mean, that was it. But I realized that if I took better care of this body of mine, it would take me further.

Recently a man asked me, "Zig, how do you find time to jog?" And I looked at him and said, "I've got so much to do, I don't have time *not* to jog." Think about it: I invest twenty-five minutes a day, five days a week, in jogging. As a result, I have increased energy and capacity that will enable me to work at least an hour and a half and probably two to two and a half hours more a day. I invest a minute, and I get three minutes back for it instantly. I've got so much to do that I do *not* have time not to run. I believe that if we invest wisely, we'll get our investment back many times over.

I'm also going to talk frankly about our *mental health*, because most of us have a mental diet that is incredibly poor.

I was listening to some motivational recordings, which were talking about the mind. One particular scientist was an expert. I have confidence that he knew exactly what he was talking about. As you know, they compare the mind to the computer. He estimated that if they could develop a computer that was equal to the human mind, the price of it would be an enormous amount of money—a minimum of at least $100 million.

We recently added a computer to our own business. Even though it is a small business, it was a fairly reasonable investment. We brought in an expert to program the computer, because the computer is no more effective than the programmer who puts the information into it.

Now, let me ask you, if you had a $100 million computer, what kind of expert would you bring in to program it? Let me tell you about what the average American brings in to program this "$100 million computer."

As you know, people often refer to the age of two as the "terrible twos." Here is the interesting thing: every time a brand-new baby comes home, there's a proud papa, and before the young 'un gets home, Daddy has gone down to the sporting goods store, buying a baseball bat and a football helmet, and he's telling all of his friends that that little guy is already trying to date the nurse before he gets out of the hospital. If it's a girl, it's Miss America all the way—never any question about it.

By the time the child is three days old, the parents are carrying on an extended conversation about the smartest, the brightest, the most beautiful, the finest, most developed physical specimen ever known to humanity.

This goes on for about two years. Then one day, that eight-pounder grows into a twenty-pounder, starts doing a little thinking on its own, and gets out and asserts itself. Mommy and Daddy can't keep that young 'un in its place, and they don't necessarily like that anymore. So they start trying to put that young 'un back down, because they could deal with it better as an infant. This is especially true if mother and dad are a little insecure themselves, and if their self-images are not so good.

Have you ever heard your grandparents say things like, "You'd better enjoy your babies while they're babies, because one of these days, they're going to get up, and they're going to get away from you. They're going to do exactly what they want, and what you want them to do won't make any difference at all. You'd better keep them under your thumb while you've got them."

How many times have I heard that? All of a sudden, at age two, this marvelously brilliant, beautiful, athletically endowed child begins to change. Now the negative input begins to enter into that child's life.

I came home one night, and my daughter and her two-year-old daughter were there. When I walked in the front door, my grandbaby looked up and said, "There's Grandy." And she took off in a dead run for the front door. She was a magnificent specimen of femininity. Gorgeous, long, blond hair: any shampoo company in the world would be way ahead of the game if they could just get her endorsement. A personality that would go over big on any television program, and intelligence that Einstein himself would have been envious of. (You parents and grandparents will recognize the validity and appreciate the honesty of my evaluation, telling things exactly as they are.) She came running to me. I grabbed her, threw her up in the air, and caught her. She hugged my neck, gave me a big kiss, reared back, and said, "I love my Grandy."

Now can you imagine the audacity of anybody saying "terrible twos"? They're the terrific twos. They're the tremendous threes. They're the fabulous fours. They're the fantastic fives. They're the super sixes. They are sensational sevens. But what is the input into the mind? Remember, you can't plant negative thoughts and raise positive kids.

I was in the Nashville Airport once, on the way to the gate to catch a plane. I walked past a mother and her little five-year-old son. As mothers well know, there has never been a child since Adam and Eve who walked at exactly the right speed. As I walked past them, she turned to him and said, "Come on, stupid. We're going to miss the plane."

We were in a cafeteria in Dallas once. A pretty little seven-year-old blond girl in front of us was crying. A grandmotherly lady leaned down and said, "What's the matter, honey?" The girl's daddy said, "She's mean. That's what. She's just plain mean."

If these two parents came to me and asked, "Zig, what would you suggest that we do to make absolutely certain that we destroy the self-image and the confidence of our children?" I'd reply, "Keep it up. That's all. Just keep it up."

So many times, we reinforce the negative. A little guy comes home from school. There were thirty questions on the test, and he gets twenty-seven of them right and three of them wrong. What do most of the parents zero in on? "Honey, didn't you know that?"

Another little boy comes home from school and says, "Dad, I'm afraid I flunked the arithmetic test." His dad said, "Don't sweat it, son; honestly, I never could learn this stuff either." The negativity is incredible.

A little girl is trying to help mom with the dishes and drops one. Mother makes a statement like, "You're always dropping things." But there's a vast difference between dropping a dish and *always* dropping a dish.

A little boy goes out, and one of his parents says, "Johnny, tuck your shirttail in. You never look nice." But there's a lot of difference between having your shirttail out once and never looking nice.

Let me tell you something: whatever you put in is going to come out. Let me remind you of some of the statements that people make. A housewife gets up, looks at the house, and says, "Boy, I'll never get this mess cleaned up." An overweight person sits down at the table and says, "Everything I eat turns to fat." A mother sends her child off to school and says, "Now don't you get run over."

Our terminology is negative. Somebody brings out a fresh loaf of bread and takes one slice off it, and what do they call the very first slice? The end. Why? It's the beginning.

Even the weatherman gets in on the act. He comes on the TV screen and says, "We've got a 40 percent chance of rain." Why doesn't the dirty dog tell me we've got a 60 percent chance of sunshine?

Probably the greatest damage that the white man has done to his black brother has to do with self-image. On one program, Bill Cosby showed a Shirley Temple movie from the 1930s. When I was a boy, I used to go to Shirley Temple movies to see Little Miss Perfect sing "On the Good Ship Lollipop," but I want you to look at that movie today through a different set of eyes. It will help us understand the causes of some of the problems that are so easily solved once we get our hearts in the right place.

In this picture, Shirley Temple is having a birthday party. She's five years old. The birthday party is just about over. A little black girl, around fourteen years old, comes to the front of the house with several of her little buddies, and she says, "Miss Shirley, we've got a birthday present for you." And Miss Shirley says, "Thank you very much! We have some birthday cake left, so why don't you come on in and have a piece of our leftover birthday cake?"

The fourteen-year-old black girl drops her head, starts to cry, and says, "Oh, Miss Shirley!"

As I looked at that clip, for the first time I realized the enormous impact of the importance of a healthy self-image. In recent years, black people have come further, faster than ever before. I believe that it's primarily because of a change of the image that they have of themselves.

You see, when we understand that the color of our skin has nothing whatever to do with the ability and with the heart that's inside of the individual, we begin to place the proper emphasis on what image really is all about.

You see what I'm getting at. The programing that we enforce upon our children is amazing. Most of us wake up with the aid of an electronic rooster. What do they call that electronic rooster? An alarm clock. You hear an alarm when they're robbing a bank or there's a fire going on. If people wake up scared to death, it's no wonder they end up being negative. Truth of the matter is, it's an opportunity clock, because it means you've got an opportunity to get up. Now, friend, if you don't hear it, that means you've just lost that opportunity.

In short, the conversation is essentially negative, so the programming of this computer is amazing. It's amazing how many people bring in experts who are anything but experts to run their lives.

In the average American family, the television is on six hours and fifty minutes a day, and the average American watches television four hours every day. By the time they've graduated from high school, your teenage son or daughter will have witnessed thirteen thousand violent murders and over forty thousand rapes. They have witnessed over a quarter of a million devastating acts of violence. They've heard millions of profane, obscene words.

We wonder sometimes why we have so much teenage burglary, so much homicide, so much rape. We wonder why there is so much illegitimacy, so many pregnancies, so much venereal disease. You know what I wonder? I wonder why there's not more.

As the Good Book says, "As you sow, so shall you reap" (Galatians 6:7). You don't even have to believe that in order for it to be a fact. It's like the law of gravity. If you step off the roof of a twenty-story building, it doesn't make a bit of difference whether you believe in the law of gravity or not. A thousand times out of a thousand, down you're going to come. We're glad it works every time, aren't we? Wouldn't it be frustrating to get up every morning, stick your foot out the side of the bed, and wonder, is it going to go down or up?

Why do I talk about this? Because whatever has been programmed into our mind on a negative basis can be reversed: we can begin to program it on a positive basis.

In our society, we've been conditioned to believe a lot of ridiculous things. Take cigarette ads. They suggest that if you smoke, you're more masculine or feminine: it improves your sex appeal. What they're really saying is, "Look, all you've got to do is smoke me, and never again will any member of the opposite sex be able to say no to you." This is so effective that each year, billions and billions of cigarettes are sold.

Does smoking cigarettes really make you more attractive to members of the opposite sex? Think about it for a moment. When you kiss somebody who's been smoking, it's like licking an ashtray. But people have been conditioned to believe otherwise, so down to the store they go, and buy them by the billions, every single year.

Then there is this commercial. The sun is setting. A beautiful boat is out at sea. A deep, resonant voice comes on: "Now that the catch is in, now comes Miller time." Or this one: "You go through life only once. Go through it with all the gusto you can." You watch athletes, the epitome of health, sell booze as being good for you. In movies, whether it's the good guy or the bad guy, when he is confronted with a crisis, he takes a drink. When you're confronted with a problem, take a drink. When you're in a social situation, it is considered poor taste not to have a drink around. It's gracious living. It's relaxation. It's fun.

Now that's what the commercials say. What do the drinkers say? Being smashed sounds like fun. The sound of your gourd knocked under the table sounds like fun.

Now you might say, "Yeah, but those are for the guys who overdo it. How about the ones who just have a drink?" We know that one person out of fourteen who takes a drink will become an alcoholic, and that's kind of frightening. Here's a figure. Over 50 percent of the people who are under the care of a psychiatric professional are suffering from depression or are there as a direct result of alcohol.

We've been conditioned to believe that one person cannot make any difference in the overall picture. But don't even try to sell that idea to Lori Cox from Scottsdale, Arizona. Lori had the idea that we really should be saying the Pledge of Allegiance and saluting the flag of the United States of America in schools. She went to her teacher and suggested that idea, and the teacher thought that Lori was off base. Lori went to the principal and said we should be saying the Pledge of Allegiance and saluting the flag, and the principal thought Lori was a little bit kooky.

Lori then went to every student at Coronado High School in Scottsdale, Arizona, and got three thousand signatures. Lori believed that if you saluted the flag as a child, then, when the need arose, you would not only be willing to serve and defend that flag but would be anxious to do it.

One person makes a difference. If you don't believe it's you, just think about a couple of guys named Jay Van Andel and Rich DeVos, the founders of Amway. When they started, they could have held their national sales meeting in your bathroom. Today, the company does billions of dollars of business a year.

Friends, let me tell you what $1 billion really means. A billion dollars means over $500 million in profits. What does $500 million in profits translate to? It translates into thousands of magnificent homes. It translates into hundreds of thousands of straight teeth and well-clothed bodies. It translates into college educations for youngsters who otherwise never would have had them. It means the divorcée, the widow, the elderly couple, the senior citizen is able to maintain their dignity and work right as long as they want to and realize an incredible income. That's what that kind of business translates into.

So you get carried away with that big old figure, and it doesn't mean anything until you see some-body who's never really taken a nice trip, driven a nice car, had a marvelous vacation, or been able to buy their wife a nice diamond ring or a fur coat.

Just for a moment let's play a game. Let's pretend that your telephone rings tomorrow morning. The voice on the other end says, "John, I know you don't want be disturbed. I haven't called to ask a favor. As a matter of fact, I have called to say something to you that I should have many months ago. You see, John, I happen to think you're one of the nicest guys who ever drew a breath of air. You're an asset to your com-munity. You're a credit to your profession. You're the kind of man that I like to spend time with, because when I'm with you and around you, I'm always excited, I'm enthused, I'm motivated, I'm inspired, I'm turned on. If I could spend ten minutes a day with you, I could turn this world upside down, because you are the kind of guy that motivates me. Although, I've known you for many years, this is the first time I've ever expressed my appreciation to you as an indi-vidual. I just wanted to call you, John, and let you know that I have great admiration for you and look forward to seeing you again soon." Then he hangs up.

Suppose that you had received the telephone call like that. Suppose that you knew for a fact that it was from an old, established, and trusted friend. Suppose there was no question in your mind about his sincerity; you knew that he was leveling with you. May I ask you, what kind of a day would you have?

If you were raising kids, wouldn't you be a better mother or a father? If you were pulling teeth, if you were a schoolteacher, if you were a ditch digger, if you were closing sales, do you believe that, regardless of what you happen to be doing that day, you would be better at it?

How much more would you know about your profession? How much more would you know about pulling teeth or closing sales, raising kids, or educating your family? How much more would you know about being a mother or a father? The answer is obvious: you would know nothing more.

You would be better because you had a change of image. You'd say, "I'm a credit to my profession. That old boy said so, and he is one smart cookie."

Very simply, your self-image determines your performance. I believe that you can build a ship in the Sahara if you have the right attitude about your self-image.

The greatest thing you can do for anybody is not to give them part of what you've got, but to reveal to that individual what he or she has. The story of Victor Serebriakoff says exactly what I want to say. When he was a young man of about fifteen years, his teacher said to him, "Victor, you're a dunce. Why don't you drop out of school? You're never going to make it. Why don't you get a job and learn a trade.

Then maybe by the time you're an adult, you'll be able at least to support yourself."

Here's the voice of authority. The teacher told him, "You're a dunce," and Victor Serebriakoff in effect said, "Yes, ma'am" or "Yes, sir." He dropped out of school. He became an itinerant. Over a period of the next seventeen years, he did 101 different things, none of them very well.

When Victor Serebriakoff was thirty-one or thirty-two years old, someone did a psychological evaluation of him and made an astonishing discovery. They discovered that he had an IQ of 161.

You are what you believe you are. For seventeen years, Victor had been getting up every morning and dressing a dunce. For seventeen years, he had been going to work as a dunce. For seventeen years, he had been going to the dunce's pay window and receiving a dunce's wages.

Now, all of a sudden, without any increase in knowledge, without acquiring anything different, he now learned that instead of a dunce, he was in fact a genius. He started getting up in the morning and shaving a genius, dressing a genius, going to work as a genius, and performing as a genius, because you perform as you see yourself.

The results were dramatic. After that, Victor Serebriakoff wrote several books and patented a number of inventions. He was an enormously successful businessman and was elected as international chairman of Mensa, the society for people with a high IQ. You must have an IQ of at least 132 in order to be a member of Mensa.

Let's learn from Babe Ruth. He struck out more times than any man in baseball history, but most of us do not remember him as a failure. Ty Cobb was thrown out when stealing base more than any other man in history. We don't think of him as a failure. Thomas Edison failed over ten thousand times on one experiment. We don't think of him as a failure. Vince Lombardi was forty-four years old, and the offensive coordinator coach for the New York Giants, before he had his opportunity to go coach Green Bay. Enrico Caruso's voice failed so many times when he hit the high note that his teacher said that he would never make it. Albert Einstein flunked a course in math. Wernher von Braun did exactly the same thing. These men failed, but they kept on because they discovered something that's critically important: the only difference between a big shot and a little shot is that a big shot is just a little shot that kept shooting.

If we want to make it big in life, we need to learn from these successful failures. You can step up to the plate and strike out, step up to the plate and strike out, and step up to the plate and strike out, and boom! You clear the bases.

I'm talking about building a healthy self-image. I'm not talking about acquiring a super-inflated "I am the greatest" kind of ego. You know, conceit is a weird disease, isn't it? It makes everybody sick except the one that's got it.

Yes, your self-image is tremendously important. As a matter of fact, the late Dr. Maxwell Maltz said that the goal of any form of psychotherapy was to change the self-image of the individual.

A lot of people say, "I can't remember names." They think they're inferior because they can't remember everybody they meet and everything that they see or hear. Saying that an ability to remember a lot of people means a person has a great mind is like saying a dictionary is a great piece of literature.

Actually, I believe that the person who can't forget is infinitely worse off than the individual who can't remember everything that they hear.

Having said that, let me also say that a poor memory is a matter of choice. If you want a super memory, there are marvelous series of books that will teach you exactly how to develop it.

Many people have a poor self-image because they make the mistake of comparing experiences. They figure that because somebody else can do something they can't do, that individual has got to be superior. But as you know, there are hundreds of millions of Chinese children who can do something that you and I can't do: speak Chinese. Does that make those children smarter than we are? I don't think so. I think what that really says is they've had a different experience.

There are millions of Australians who can do something that you and I can't do: they can drive down the left-hand side of the highway. Does that mean that they have a superior intellect? Not at all. It simply means that they have a different experience than the experience that we have had.

Let me give you another example. Once, for some wild reason, coming home one evening, I decided that I was going to drive down our alley, even though it had been raining, and our alley had not been paved.

Lo and behold, what did I do? I got stuck right in the back of my own house. I wrestled with that car. I burned rubber for about five or ten minutes. I tried as much as I knew how to get that car out. Finally, I realized that nobody else was going to come down the alley that night, so I just left it.

The next morning, I got up, went back out to my car, and took some sand, gravel, bricks, and boards. I burned a lot more rubber. Finally, after about another fifteen or twenty minutes, I gave up and called the tow truck.

The tow truck came out, and the man looked at the car. Judging from his conversation, I would estimate that he probably got past the second day of the first grade. He had absolutely no education, but he looked at that car for a moment and said, "Let me see your keys."

"What do you want with them?"

"I believe I can drive it out of there."

I said, "Man, there ain't no way. I've already burned enough rubber to drive ten thousand miles, and I don't want to burn any more."

"Just let me give it a try."

I decided I'd be very gracious about it. I was going to let him give him a try, and then I wasn't going to rub it in when he obviously could not. I was going to say, "Well, you know, we all just have to try."

The man sits down, cranks the car, turns the wheel, and revs it twice. It must have taken him every bit of fifteen seconds to drive it out of that mud hole.

I said, "Where in the world did you learn how to do that? I'm flabbergasted."

He grinned and said, "To tell you the truth, I was raised in East Texas. I've been driving out of bigger mudholes than that since I was twelve years old."

To build your self-image, make a victory list. Start it from the time you were four or five years old. List all of the things that you've done, like getting an A in a class they said you could not pass. If you ever get a little bit down, pull the list out, read it, and say, "You know, a person that can do all these things can't be all bad."

You must decide: are you *for* you or *against* you? If we are going to build our healthy self-image or make it a healthier one, we need to learn in life from the successful failures.

The third kind of health that I'm going to discuss is *spiritual health*. You know that you're probably not going to live to be 120 years old, but your soul will live forever. Therefore, to develop only that part of you that is going to live seventy-five or a hundred years and to ignore that part which will live forever seems like a terrible mistake.

I'm also going to talk about money because I believe money is important. I don't know about you, but I've had it and I haven't had it, and I can tell you from personal experience, it's better to have it.

Most people don't understand money. They talk about cold, hard cash, and that's crazy. It's neither cold nor hard. It's very soft, very warm. It's amazing, how many people have been improperly conditioned about money. They talk about it as if it's something bad to have.

I've got news for you. The Bible talks more about success than it does heaven. There are over seven hundred direct references to money in the Bible. Some of my Christian friends occasionally ask me, "How do you reconcile all that talk about money with Christianity?" I grin and say, "It's easy. I think God made the diamonds for his crowd, not for Satan's bunch. My Bible tells me that Jacob was a millionaire, that Moses was a millionaire, that Abraham had more cattle than the loudest Texan. It tells me that Solomon was the richest man who ever lived. Even old Job wouldn't qualify for the food stamp program, if you know what I mean."

There's nothing wrong with money. Get as much as you want; just don't let the money get you.

I also want to talk about happiness, because many people have not the slightest concept about it. They think happiness is a where and a when and that it belongs to somebody else. A lot of people say, "I'll be happy when I get the house." No way. "I'll be happy when I've got the new furniture." Uh-uh. "I'll be happy when I get the mortgage paid off." Happiness is not a where or a when.

Let me tell you how to instantly become a great deal happier than you are at this moment. Close your eyes and imagine that every material thing on the face of this earth that you now have has suddenly been taken away from you. Every human being on the face of this earth that you love has been suddenly taken away from you. Imagine that just for a second. Now imagine that all of a sudden, you got them back.

Makes all the difference in the world, doesn't it? We need to count all of the good things we have right now, and that will make us a whole lot happier.

There is something else that a lot of people want: peace of mind. See, I happen to believe you can get all these things. I believe health, wealth, happiness, peace of mind, friends, security, personal growth— all those things—are available. Yes, I'm an optimist. I'm the kind of guy who would go after Moby Dick in a rowboat and take the tartar sauce with me.

I believe that all these things are available to you. I believe that peace of mind is available, too, but I believe that the only way we will obtain it will be to resolve the question of eternity. When that issue is properly resolved in our minds, peace of mind is within reach.

A lot of people say, "I want to have more security." A lot of people think security is in a bank account. No, it's not. I've got a good friend who lost a million dollars. A lot people think it comes with a position. No, it's not that. You can even get to be the president of the United States, but if you don't do well, they'll get you out of that job, too. Security is in your ability to produce, grow, and land on your feet. Security is the ability to see the right side, the good side, of life.

Some people say, "I would like to have more friends." In this book, I'm not going to talk a whole lot about winning friends and influencing people. I do believe that by the time we get through, you will have more friends, because you're going to be a lot friendlier with yourself—and that's where friendships really start.

I have to add that most people are happy only when they're growing. As a result of the work I do with a lot of companies, I can tell you emphatically that people are more inclined to be loyal to a company where they're growing—where they have growth opportunities, a positive moral atmosphere and environment, and shared excitement, love, joy, and enthusiasm.

TWO

A Solid Foundation

I n the previous chapter, I talked about different kinds of health. I also talked about happiness and success as I believe they really are.

I'm convinced that in order to get those things, you have to have a solid foundation. If you go to downtown Dallas, Chicago, New York, or Los Angeles, you will see all of the excavations where they're preparing to build buildings. A good engineer can look at the depth and the width of the hole and tell you how big and tall the building is going to be.

Similarly, I can look at the foundation upon which you build your family, your business, and your personal life, and I can tell you what kind of life and what kind of family you're going to have. The foundation is the key. If you don't have that foundation in proper order, you're going to come up short.

The foundation starts with honesty, character, and integrity. Those are three of the building blocks. I did a survey of twelve of America's leading business-people. One of them was the chairman of the board of the Coca-Cola Company. I asked them, what do you consider the foundation stones for going to the top and staying there? They all agreed that you've got to build that foundation on honesty, character, and integrity.

They throw in another word: motivation. We're all born to win, but the problem is we've been conditioned to lose. If you're going to win, you've got to add in motivation.

There's a story about a rich West Texan who had a beautiful daughter of marriageable age, and he decided to do a little group prospecting. He sent out invitations to all the young men within a hundred miles of his magnificent estate. This estate had thousands of acres of land, dozens of producing oil wells, and an Olympic-size swimming pool.

The rich Texan entertained them into that evening. About midnight, he invited them out by the swimming pool, which he had the foresight to stock with water moccasins and alligators. He said, "Fellows, to the first one of you guys who will jump in this pool and swim the length of it, I'm going to give you a choice of three things: Number one, a million dollars in cash. Number two, ten thousand acres of my very best land, including the land upon which this home is built. Or number three, the hand of my beautiful daughter in marriage, and I think it's obvious that she's our only heir. The man who gets her will get everything we have."

No sooner were the words out of his mouth then there was a loud splash in that Olympic-size pool, followed almost instantly by the emergence of a dripping young man from the other end who had just set a world's record that will never be touched by anybody.

The host was excited. He ran down to the other end and said, "Son, that's fantastic. You've won. Do you want the million dollars?"

The young man said, "No, sir."

"Well, would you like the ten thousand acres of my very best land?"

"No, sir."

"Then, son, I've got to assume that what you really want is the hand of my beautiful daughter in marriage."

"No, sir."

"Then, son, for crying out loud, what do you want?"

"I want to know the name of the guy who pushed me in the pool."

I would add three other things to that foundation: faith, love, and loyalty. We have a lot of difficulty in our great land today. There are possibilities of conflict in the Middle East, Iran, all over the world. But the difficulty did not start with the current admin-istration or even the one before that. It started right after World War II, when we began to feel guilty about our strength, our wealth, and all of the blessings God had given us as a nation. We were made to feel guilty by a lot of people, and we started destroying our mil-itary might and superiority. We also started straying from the things upon which our country was built: honesty, character, integrity, and faith in Almighty God. That's when our difficulty really started.

Many parents today will preach to their children, "Tell the truth," but when the telephone rings, they say, "Tell them I'm not home." A parent will say, "Obey the law," but they have a radar detector in their car. The child interprets that to mean, "Look, kid, if you're going to break the law, don't be a dumb bunny and get caught."

I've been in the drug war for a number of years, and I can't tell you the number of parents that I've dealt with. Some of them have been sitting there, weeping bitter tears, some of them angry, some of them frustrated, all of them concerned. They would say, "I don't know how that kid got off on smoking that dope and popping those pills. That's the craziest thing I've ever heard of. We give them everything, and they do a dumb thing like that." But I tell the parent that the child cannot distinguish between the cocktail or beer in your hand and the reefer in his hand.

A parent will say, "OK, son, you can go to the movie; just tell them you're eleven years old. We both know you're thirteen, but you're small. They can't tell the difference." When a parent does that, they shouldn't be surprised when three years later, the child is arrested for shoplifting—they taught them that it's all right to cheat as long as you don't get caught at it.

My mama used to say to me that she couldn't be a little bit pregnant: she either was or wasn't. She'd also say that when you break an egg, you never have to doubt whether it's fresh or rotten. When that egg is rotten, you'll know it. It's the same thing when credibility is destroyed. When your children start putting question marks after what you say, that is the moment your effectiveness is dramatically reduced.

My good friend Cavett Robert said that character is the ability to carry out a good resolution long after the excitement of the moment has passed. You may go to a workshop for a weekend and you're excited, but what are you going to do on Monday morning? That's character.

Many people are confused about what motivation and positive thinking are as opposed to positive believing. Positive thinking is the optimistic hope, not necessarily based on any facts, that you can move mountains. Positive believing is the same optimistic hope, but this time based on a reason for believing it.

Let me give you a ridiculous example. A talk show host on national television asked me, "Do you think you can do anything? For example, do you think you could whip Muhammad Ali with positive thinking?"

I said, "Friend, I don't care how positive I've gotten, I never could whip Muhammad Ali. I'm too old. I'm too fat. I'm too slow. I'm too scared. I have a low threshold of pain. Besides, the guy never bothered me. Why should I want to whip him? But if I really thought I could, if I were convinced down to the very core of my being, then maybe I would last twenty seconds instead of just fifteen."

Positive believing is the same as optimistic hope, but this time based on a reason for believing that you can do it. If Larry Holmes were to say, "I believe I can whip Muhammad Ali," you could say he has legitimate reasons for believing it. After all, he's a heavyweight champion, and he's younger than Ali.

When you really develop character, you have good reasons for believing that you can do marvelous things.

What's integrity? Let me tell you about integrity. I saw it demonstrated magnificently years ago, in a Schwinn bicycle shop in Dallas. My son and I went in to buy a bicycle. We had to wait because a grandmother was there with her grandson. She had a list of exactly what she wanted for her grandson's bicycle, and she told the owner, "I want this."

The owner looked at her and said, "I've got that exact bicycle; who is it for?"

"It's for my grandson."

"Well, you want this bicycle, all right, but you want it in a much smaller size."

The lady said, "No. I want exactly the best. I want the same thing the boy across the street has."

"Well, ma'am," said the owner, "this is exactly the same thing, but a bicycle this size is much too large for your grandson. You need a smaller size."

"Absolutely not. I want the best. I want this one right over here. I want the same thing the boy across the street has."

Again the owner tried to explain to the grandmother, but she was adamant. The owner looked at her dead center and said, "Ma'am, you're probably going to think I'm crazy when I say this, but I can't sell you that bicycle for your grandson. He's much too small. He could never control it. It would be dangerous for him to leave here with that bicycle. He would fall, and if he were in the street, he might well fall in front of a car and get hurt, maybe even killed. I could never sleep again knowing that I had contributed to that."

The grandmother left in a huff.

You might say, "Zig, is that taking it too far?" No, absolutely not. You see, I believe you can get everything you want in life if you help enough other people to get what they want. Although the man missed a sale right there, I would send my son into that shop today without a question with a signed blank check, and I would say, "Son, whatever the man says to you, that's exactly what you ought to get."

That's the value of integrity. That's what you build your business on. That enables you to face every person tomorrow as you face them today.

I've also got to have a thing called faith. I don't know you, the reader, as a person. I have no idea who you might be. I don't know how old or young or rich or strong you are. I don't know about your race, your creed, or your color. I don't know how wealthy or how poor you are, but there's one thing I know with absolute certainty about you: if you already haven't had it, the day will come when you will have a situation that human resources simply cannot deal with.

That's where faith enters the picture. I'd still have great faith if I'd never heard a preacher preach or if I'd never opened up my Bible, if all I'd done had been working with kids on drugs. Because I've seen not one or a dozen but hundreds of them, working with programs that follow the same basic procedures as Alcoholics Anonymous. Number one, recognize that you've got a problem. Number two, accept the fact that you can't do anything about it. Number three, realize that you need a higher source for the solution of the problem—God, as you understand him. I'm so grateful that I don't have to say just God as I understand him, but Jesus Christ as I know him. That make all the difference in the world.

Then you need to have love in your life. One of the most intriguing things about love is that most of us don't have models to go by. We've only seen imitations.

Recently I spoke to a group of bankers. I pointed this out, and got the nod of agreement from all of the bankers there: when they teach you to be a teller in a bank, they don't run a lot of counterfeit money by you. As a matter of fact, they don't run *any* counterfeit money by you. They don't want you to see it, smell it, or anything else. They want it to be nonexistent. Every day, they want you simply to see the genuine article over and over, so the instant a counterfeit hits your hand, you know it just like that, because you've been dealing with the real thing.

In the case of love, many of our youngsters have never seen anything but the pornographic display of lust in the magazines, on television, and in the movie theater. They've never seen a mother and a father who really love and hug and kiss and deeply care for each other.

The theater marquee says, "The Most Beautiful Love Story Ever Told." Someday, somebody somewhere is going to tell the most beautiful human love story ever told. Even so, that's all it will be—just the most beautiful human love story ever *told*. It will not be the most beautiful love story ever. Those stories will never be told. They're lived quietly by thousands of people like you. You see, no man or woman deeply committed to each other in the bonds of holy matrimony would ever dream of revealing the essence of that love to even one human being, because to do so would make it common, and nothing common is really beautiful.

You know what our country needs? It needs to have millions of youngsters see millions of parents unashamedly demonstrating care and love and affection for each other, so when the youngsters see the genuine article, they'll recognize immediately what it's all about. If we teach our kids what love really is, we can put a stop to much of what is happening in our country today. We've got to quit saying, "Why don't they do something?" and say, "Here's what I'm doing every day to make it better." It's been rightly said that if everybody cleaned up his own doorstep, we'd have a clean America.

The other part of the foundation has to do with loyalty, which really is part of the same thing. I do a lot of traveling. I've traveled over three million miles, and I've met just about every kind of human being on the face of this earth. For sixteen years, I knocked on doors. I've been in every kind of home our country has to offer. I've spent the night in homes worth millions, and I've been in homes where I could look through the floor and see the ground underneath and look through the roof and see the stars outside. I've dealt with every race, creed, and color. I've crossed every ethnic line and every socioeconomic barrier this country has to offer. I've dealt with them all. In all of my life, I have never known a happy man or a happy woman who was married who was not loyal to their mate. Period.

Folks, I'm not preaching. I'm simply saying to you that if you want happiness in life and you're married, you have no choice: you must be loyal to your mate. I've seen a lot of people laugh and cut up and carry on, but I've never seen one of them, who, when we really explore the depths of their feeling, have been happy. Loyalty is an absolute must.

You may be saying now, "Zig, doggone it. Wait just a minute, man. I have honesty, character, integrity, faith, love, and loyalty, and I'm stone broke. How do explain that?"

In the first place, I think of the Chinese bamboo tree. You know the story: They plant the seed. They water it. They fertilize it. The first year, nothing happens. The next year, they water and fertilize it, and nothing happens. The next year, they water and fertilize it again, and still nothing happens. The same thing happens in the fourth year. Sometime during the fifth year, the bamboo tree grows ninety feet in approximately six weeks. But did it grow ninety feet in six weeks, or did it grow ninety feet in five years? Obviously the latter, because had you failed to water or fertilize in any one of those years, there would have been no Chinese bamboo tree.

The difference is character. You hang in there. A postage stamp is judged entirely by its ability to stick to the job until it gets there.

Furthermore, a lot of people build a marvelous foundation and then proceed to erect a chicken shack on it. If you're going to build a chicken shack, you're going to have to live in a chicken shack, and that's tragic. Many people have misused their imagination. They imagine the things they *don't* want to happen, and then of course they do. We see it every day.

Once I was doing some filming down in Dallas. A little lady was seated on the front row. She had a Dr Pepper on her hand. She slipped it under a chair and said out loud, "Now watch I'll spill this."

Is that what she wanted to happen, or is that what she didn't want to happen? You would think she wanted it to happen. She asked for it, did she not?

Or you watch somebody show up for work, and they've got a little sniffle. Somebody says, "I see you've got a sniffle." They say, "Yeah, but it's just the first day. It doesn't really get bad until the third day. That's when it kills me."

You ask somebody, "How are you doing?" They say, "I've just got a little headache, but they don't really get bad until about three in the afternoon." And they're amazed when they do feel awful at three in the afternoon. We ask for what we don't want.

With all this, I'm really talking about a very practical approach to life. With this kind of foundation, you can get all of the things you want—health, wealth, and happiness.

THREE

Six Steps for Reaching Your Objectives

As we begin to build our foundation, we've got to take some steps which are really fairly simple. We've got to start with self-image.

Dr. David McClelland at Harvard spent twenty-five years on the subject and came to the inescapable conclusion that before you can improve your performance, you must improve the way you see yourself. Your self-image is critically important. There's no question about it.

You also need to establish winning relationships with others, which is easy to do after you've built up your self-image. You don't go through life by yourself. You don't climb the high mountain by yourself. Other people are involved. As I've said over and over, you can get everything you want in life if you just help enough other people get what they want.

Obviously, you've also got to set goals. Ninety-seven percent of the people in our country never take all of the six steps that you must take in order to reach their objectives in life. The six steps are:

1. Carefully identify what you want.
2. Put a time limit on when you expect to get there.
3. List and identify the obstacles you have to overcome.
4. Find out what you've got to know and how much you've got to grow.
5. List the people, groups, and organizations you need to work with.
6. Answer the question, what's in it for me? What are the benefits that come my way?

That's where your dreams come in. A beautiful thing about life is that we can dream those dreams, and we can make those dreams come true.

In addition, you've got to have the right mental attitude. Let me go back to that computer, that magnificent, $100 million mind of yours. We do not want to turn it over to just anybody; we need to feed it good, clean, pure, powerful, positive food every day. From your neck down, you're worth about a hundred bucks a week. From the neck up, there's no limit to what you're worth. You feed the hundred-dollar a week part regularly; why not feed the hundred-million-dollar part just as often? Let me say it again:

you would feed that million-dollar race horse carefully. You need to feed your body carefully, and the body starts at the top of your head and goes right down to the tip of your toes. You need to eat the right mental food.

Of course you also have to work, but I'm not going to talk very much about work in this book. That doesn't mean I'm trying to play it down, because I'm not. I absolutely believe that more people fail because they do not persistently develop good work habits than for any other reason. Even so, I believe that if you've got the right self-image, if you've identified your goals, if you've got the right mental attitude, nobody is going to have to tell you to go to work. You're going to do the work.

I don't want to be negative. As a matter of fact, I won't be negative. I'd be like the little boy who came from school and said, "Dad, I'm afraid I flunked arithmetic test." His dad said, "Son, that's negative. Be positive." The boy said, "Dad, I'm positive I flunked the arithmetic test."

Once I had the privilege of meeting a man named Jerry Roth. Jerry is forty-two years old, and he never finished high school, but he is worth $15 million. As I talked to Jerry and some of his people, I discovered that he was probably the firmest, most demanding employer any of them have ever had. But they liked the work for one simple reason: Jerry Roth never asked them to do anything he didn't do himself and didn't do more of. He's harder on himself than he is on them, and here is the payoff: sixty-two of the people who worked for him are now in business for themselves. Twelve of them are already millionaires, even though eight of them never finished high school.

Yes, it takes a great deal of effort, but it gets exciting when you understand that you don't pay the price for success; you enjoy the results. In this entire book, you'll never see me use the word *easy*. I'm going to tell you it's fun. I'm going to tell you it's rewarding. I'm going to tell you it's exciting. But not once will I ever use the word *easy*, because I don't necessarily believe that it is. It does require some work, and yes, you really have got to desire that success.

We've identified health, wealth, and happiness as major goals. I believe that you can get all these things if you build on the right foundation and take the right steps. I also happen to believe that if you make millions of dollars and go all the way to the top but alienate your family, you're not successful.

A lot of times, people get confused. They think of success only in terms of dollars. They'll say, "Zig, the richest man in town is the biggest crook there is." OK, maybe he is the richest man in town, but how is his mental and emotional and spiritual health? How many friends does he have? How much peace of mind does he have? What enjoyment does he really get out of living? It's nice to have money, but if you've got to buy the money at the price of the others, no, it's not nice to have the money. I want the money, friends, a good family, peace of mind, and security, and I'm telling you, it's all available. Jesus Christ himself said, "I have come that you might have life and that you might have it more abundantly" (John 10:10).

Then, no question about it, you've got to live and work in a free enterprise society, where you can absolutely be free to explore and expand without undue government restraint.

You may say, "OK, Zig. I understand that you've got the right foundation, and these are the steps you've got to take. Where do we get started?"

Years ago, I heard a philosopher say, you're where you are because that's exactly where you want to be. I took that statement in. I thought, "Boy, that sounds like the truth to me. I'm going to run around the country telling everybody, you are where you are because that's exactly where you want to be."

Then one night I was in Birmingham, Alabama, on my way to Meridian, Mississippi, where I had to be early the next morning. The roads were under repair. I stopped at a service station to get directions. The attendant not only gave me the directions but drew me a little map. He said, "If you will follow these directions exactly as we have laid them out, you'll have no difficulty." One hour later, I was forty-five miles further from Meridian than I had been when I got the directions. That wasn't where I wanted to be. I was tired and sleepy. I wanted to be home. I was there because that dude had given me the wrong directions.

If you are not as far up the ladder as you want to be, if you're not as happy as you want to be, maybe it's because you've been listening to the wrong input. Maybe the programmer who's been putting those can't-do, low-ceiling concepts into your mind has had an impact on your life.

At this point, we are flat out going to eliminate all the garbage dump thinking by properly programming what we want in the future.

When I talk about garbage, I'm thinking about a large Southern city, where there is a beautiful new shopping center. About thirty ago, it was the city dump. For a hundred years, they'd been dumping garbage there. Then they saw the city growing in that direction, and they stopped the dumping of garbage. They persuaded the builders to haul out loads of dirt and put it on the dump. For several years, they put thousands of loads of dirt on the old garbage dump until one day the builder came along and said, "The foundation is ready. Let's build a new shopping center," and they did. The shopping center is actually built on a foundation of garbage.

I don't care how much garbage has been dumped into your mind. I don't care how many low ceilings have been put over you, or how many people have said you can't do it—that is nothing but garbage.

You can't make an overdraft on the bank of right mental attitude all your life and then expect to bring the account up to date with one deposit. One attempt won't do it, but you can start by putting a layer of veneer over that old garbage. Then you're going to put another layer, then another layer, and another.

But if you're not very careful, if you don't get all of the treatments, you'll get around some negative people, and that old garbage will begin to break back through that veneer, and you'll have stinking thinking again.

What we have to do is make that veneer thicker and thicker until one day we bury all of the old garbage. Even when we've done so, along comes somebody, or we turn on the radio or the television, and suddenly two fresh loads of garbage have been dumped into our good, clean mind.

Now what do we do? We erase all the new garbage. We feed our mind with good, clean, pure, powerful motivational messages that say, "You can do it. You can do it. You can do it."

We'll eliminate all the loser's limps that you've ever seen. What's a loser's limp? The people who are making all excuses in life. You see it at the football game. The offensive player goes out and catches the pass behind the defensive man. The defensive man takes out in hot pursuit as the offensive man heads for the end zone. But when he gets about twenty yards from the end zone, the guy doing the chasing realizes he's not about to catch the guy with the ball. The fans realize it too. So what does the guy doing the chasing do? Pulls a limp. Everybody says, "No wonder he couldn't catch him. Look, he is crippled. He is hurt." That was his excuse. What's yours?

Some people say, "I'm too old." Some say, "I'm too young. They won't listen to the young people." Others say, "I was born on the wrong side of the tracks." There are some who blame one thing, some who blame another. Some even say, "I was born under the wrong star." Then there's the brand-new one: "They don't hire anybody who's not a member of a minority race or a woman. If you're not one of those, you don't have a chance." A lot of people say, "I was overqualified; that's why they didn't give me the job."

A lot of people say it was her fault and his fault and their fault, and some of them just blame everybody. But I want you to know this: when you've got one finger pointed that way, you've got three times that many fingers pointed right back at you.

We as individuals need to recognize our ability and accept the responsibility for our conduct and our performance, understanding that many people with far less than we've got have done far more. If we look at the right role models—the people who are doing it, and not those who are not doing it—if we look for the good instead of looking for the bad, if we keep seeking and dreaming and believing and working, then we will be in a magnificent position like never before.

A manager was complaining about the people where he worked. He said, "People today are more apathetic than they've ever been."

I said, "Yes. That's true, and that to me is one of the most exciting things I've ever encountered." That's because we see people who are not courteous, who are unwilling to come in a few minutes early, who are unwilling to do the extra things, who are not taking those extra steps, who don't really want to get ahead. For other people, who are willing to do the extras, who will take the extra steps, who will be a little more thoughtful, a little more courteous, who will study a little more or work a little harder, for those who are ambitious to get ahead, the opportunities today are infinitely greater than they have ever been. You can start from where you are, with what you've got, and you can realize your dream.

FOUR

The Power of Goals

M any years ago, in a cathedral in Europe, an old man sat playing at the organ. He was a superb musician. The songs were beautiful, but they had a melancholy note to them, because this was the last day that the old man was to be playing. He was being replaced by a younger man.

The following evening, as the sun was setting and its rays were settling through the beautiful stained-glass windows of the old cathedral, a young man rather brusquely stepped into the door of the cathedral. The old man saw the young man, got up, removed the key, put it in his pocket, and headed towards the door. And as he drew abreast to the young man, the young man stuck his hand out and said, "Please, sir, the key."

The old man reached in his pocket and handed the young man the key, and the young man ran to the organ. He stood in front of it for a moment. Then he sat down, turned the key, and started to play. And while the old man had played beautifully and skillfully, the young man played with sheer genius: music such as the world had never heard before came forth. It filled the cathedral. It filled the town. It filled the entire countryside. As the old man stood at the doorway listening, tears started running down his cheeks as he said to himself, "Suppose, just suppose, that I had not given the master the key."

That was the world's introduction to the music of Johann Sebastian Bach.

Just for a moment, let's play a game. Let's back your calendar up. It's a Thursday morning in January, 5:30 a.m., and the telephone rings. As you sleepily stick your hand out from under the cover, you remember that the weather report the evening before had forecast four solid inches of new snow and ice. You remember because someone had left the window open, and some of that cold wind was blowing through.

By then you're up and awake, and you've answered the phone. You become aware of the voice on the other end, and you know who he or she is. A friend of yours says, "Hey, partner. I've got fantastic news for you. I've just won a trip for four to Acapulco. We're going leave tomorrow morning at precisely 8:15 from your front lawn. A helicopter is going to come pick us up. We're going to fly out to the airport, where they're going to have a corporate jet ready for us. We're going to fly to Acapulco. We're going to stay in a millionaire's villa for four full days. We have a French chef coming in, the finest cook in the whole world; we also have an ocean-going yacht. The captain knows where all of the big fish are. For four full days, we'll have a chauffeured limousine and the best entertainment that money can buy. Everything is going to be at our disposal. The only thing I want to know is, can you and your spouse be ready to go tomorrow morning at precisely 8:15?"

Let me ask you some questions. Should you have gotten a call like that last January or if you should get one next January, do you honestly and sincerely believe that yes, you could in fact be ready to go by 8:15 the next morning?

Now you lie back down on your pillow and revel in the thought of four magnificent days out of the snow and ice, down there in the sun, where you'll have fun and games and relaxation. But then you remember, "Doggone it all, I've got that 10:30 appointment. There's no way I can get out of that, and that's going to take two hours. Oh, and I've got nine phone calls. And I've got that interview at 2:00, and that correspondence I've got to take care of."

About that time, your spouse nudges you gently in the ribs and says, "Hold it. What is this you've got to do that is so tremendously important that you would even remotely entertain the possibility that we might not go to Acapulco at somebody else's expense tomorrow morning?"

You say, "Well, honey, you know I've got that 10:30 appointment. And you know I've got to do this and that."

Your spouse jumps out of bed, grabs a pen and a sheet of paper, and says, "Now number one, what's the first thing?" And as you list them, number two, number three, number four, and so on, your spouse says, "Wait, I can take care of this one. You know the secretary can handle this one. You know your associate will take care of that one. And you've got a favor due from that one."

Do you honestly think that during the next twenty-four hours, you could get more done than you normally get done in two, three, four, even seven days?

Now let me ask you a simple question: why don't you go to Acapulco tomorrow, every day of your life, in your own mind? Because I'm talking about something you can make a reality in life as soon as you make it a reality in your own mind.

I'm talking about goals, am I not? And I'm using every one of the six steps I listed in the previous chapter (with exception of one, because this is only a short-range goal). First of all, we identified exactly where we wanted to go. Number two, we put a precise time limit on it. Number three, we listed the obstacles we had to overcome in order to get there, and number four, we enlisted the aid of other people, which is absolutely necessary if you're going to climb the high mountain. You can't do it all by yourself.

It is historically true that 97 percent of the American people do not have any objectives in their lives. That's right. They'll go to work tomorrow because that's what they did yesterday. They're what we call "wandering generalities," and there are four basic reasons why.

The first reason that most people do not have goals in life is fear. The second reason is simply that they have never been sold. Oh, they've been *told*, but they've never really been *sold*. The third reason they do not have goals is that they have such poor self-images that they do not think they deserve to succeed. The fourth reason is that nobody has ever really shown them how. If you don't know how, it is very difficult to set those goals.

Let's look at that first one: fear. Look at the way the word is spelled. It's F-E-A-R, which simply stands for *false evidence appearing real*. But if it appears real to your mind, then it's as real as if it actually existed.

When I get aboard an aircraft, I've got sense enough to know that some of those airplanes are coming down faster than they're going up. I know there's a certain amount of danger involved. But I also happen to know there's more danger for the airplane if it never leaves the ground. Engineers tell me it'll wear out or rust out faster sitting on the runway than it'll wear out flying in the heavens. Besides, flying is what airplanes are built for.

There is a danger when you set goals that you might not reach them. And then you've got to admit to yourself and to others that you did not quite make it, so you think, "Let's play it safe. Let's not set them. I don't venture anything, and therefore I risk nothing."

But according to the great playwright George Bernard Shaw, the great tragedy of life is the fact that most people take their music to their graves with them. That's a tragedy, because human beings and nature are absolutely dissimilar in one respect: You use up nature's natural resources by using them. You use up man's natural resources by not using them at all.

Surely the saddest words in the whole world are "what might have been." You see, I happen to believe deep down inside of me that every person is Spindletop. Down in Texas, we've got an oil well, and it's called Spindletop. It was brought in during a drought. The man who owned the property where Spindletop is had been having to sell off part of his property because his finances were so bad. An oil company came along and said to him, "We will pay you royalties if you will just let us drill for oil on your property." So the owner made the agreement. They brought in Spindletop, and it became the biggest gusher in the history of the oil industry, and he became an instant millionaire many times over.

We can definitely prove that the oil was there all along, but until somebody took the cap off and let it come up, they couldn't take it to market and get the value for it.

I don't care how much ability, intelligence, intellect, or talent an individual has. As long as these things stay inside, they have no marketable value. Inside of you is a Spindletop. Let's remove the fear.

Where does fear come from anyhow? We live in a world where much is conditioned, and in a very negative way. When you were an hour old, lying in the crib at the hospital, you heard some words come down the corridor: "You can't believe everything you hear." From that moment until this, you've heard those words a million times. During that same hour, you also heard these words: "Seeing is believing."

You've been conditioned all of your life to believe that if you see it, that makes it so. But look at it this way. If you and I were to witness a traffic accident at same time and the same place, and in identically the same circumstances, the chances are excellent that twenty minutes later, at least one of us would be giving a wrong report on it. Maybe both of us would be.

Seeing is not necessarily believing. If you've ever watched a magician, in five seconds he will have you believing things that absolutely are not so. You try to outfox him: "I'm going to watch the other hand. That's the way you do it; you watch the other hand." But it doesn't do you a bit of good. What you see is not necessarily what is happening in reality.

We've been conditioned to believe certain things. You can take a baby born in Shanghai, a baby born in the upper Amazon, and a baby born in Denver and put them in a crib side by side and record their babbles, and you will not be able to distinguish the babbles from each other—because all babies babble in exactly the same language. But when you raise those babies, the one from Shanghai will probably grow up believing in communism. The baby born in the upper Amazon could grow up believing in witchcraft. The baby born in Denver will obviously grow up believing in the Broncos. But if that baby is lucky enough to born into the right family, it's going to grow up believing in honesty, character, integrity, love, freedom, and free enterprise. It's going to grow up believing in equal opportunity for all and believing in all of the things that have made this country the greatest country on the face of this earth.

You are where you are and what you are because of what has gone into your mind. You can change where and what you are by changing the input into your mind.

Every action we take is preceded by an emotion. The emotion is generated by thought, and the thought is generated by the mental food that goes in to feed the thought. Let me see the food the person is feeding their mind, and I'll to tell you what they're eventually going to be doing over there, because of what goes into that mind over here. It's just as predictable as anything in the world.

We've been conditioned to believe that the dream is dead, that, even though a brand-new millionaire is created every thirty-nine minutes, opportunity no longer exists in this great land of ours. We've been conditioned to believe that we are animalistic in origin. We've been conditioned to believe that premarital and extramarital sex are perfectly all right, provided they are in a meaningful relationship. (To translate, this means, go to dinner before you go to bed.) You can be conditioned to believe just about anything, and unfortunately, much of our conditioning is negative. The beautiful thing about it is that we can reverse the conditioning, because anything that can be learned can also be unlearned.

Negativism has an impact. Bill Glass, the former all-pro end for the Cleveland Browns, does a lot of prison ministries and crusades. He and I were on a platform together, and we had a chance to visit. Bill said that over 90 percent of the prisoners repeatedly say to him they were told by their parents, "Son, one of these days, you're going to end up in jail." That's exactly right. One of the prisoners standing close by quietly said and, "You know really, I didn't disappoint my daddy. I'm exactly where he said I was going to be."

Jim Sundberg, the great catcher for the Texas Rangers and a good friend of mine was told by his daddy when he was two years old, "Son, someday you're going to grow up and be a great Major League catcher."

The great Jim Brown may have been the greatest fullback who ever lived. When he was five years old down in rural Alabama, with a perceptiveness that was astonishing for his age, he looked around and realized he did not like what he saw happening to his black brothers and sisters. He started saying, "When I'm grown up, I'm going to be the greatest fullback to ever play the game of football." In that little Alabama community, he started walking around, asking himself, "How does the greatest fullback who ever lived walk? How does the greatest fullback who ever lived talk?" The rest became history.

I don't know if you are old enough to realize this, but the older you get, the more peculiar nature gets. For example, the wind and the sun and the air begin to work hardships on bifocals after you've had them for a spell. The strength begins to leave the glass, and you have to go down and get new ones or get the old ones charged up. I'd had mine out in the sun a whole lot, and they had gotten so weak that I went down to the optometrist and got some new ones. When I walked out of the optometrist's office, all of a sudden I realized what I was doing, and then I got excited—because I realized that I'm in the business of giving people new glasses.

That's all you need, because the Spindletop is there. You've got the ability. There's no question about the opportunity. All we need is to put in the right perspective and see what is there. We need to eliminate fear. We need to move out of the negative into the positive aspects of life. If we do that, we can eliminate the things that have been causing us problems.

Let's look at eliminating that fear and then look at our goals. Do we really have to have them? You know what the major problem is with most people? They don't have direction. Oh, they're going to go to work tomorrow, because that's where they went yesterday. But if the reason for going tomorrow is just that you did it yesterday, you're not going to be as good tomorrow as you were yesterday, because now you're two days older and you're no closer to the goals (which you do not have in the first place).

Often we see people out there who are working, who are really getting after it. All of a sudden, they think, "I ought to be spending more time with my family." When they're spending time at home with their family, they think, "I ought to be out there building a business." When they're out there building a business, they are thinking, "I ought to be home." Then they say to everybody, "I don't ever have time to do anything." No wonder. They're always traveling.

I don't believe time is a difficulty; I believe that lack of direction is the major problem. In 1953, Yale University surveyed its graduating seniors. They discovered that only 3 percent of them had written their objectives down, put a time limit on how long it would take to get there, listed the obstacles they had to overcome, identified the growth process— what you've got to know—and identified the people, groups, or organizations they needed to work with. Another 10 percent had a vague idea. They knew what they what they wanted, but they didn't have a time limit or they hadn't put it all down.

Twenty years later, in 1973, Yale did a follow up study of those graduating seniors. They discovered that the 3 percent who had taken all five of the steps had accomplished more than the 97 percent who had not. You've got to have goals. You can't make it a wandering generality. You must be specific.

Several years ago I was flying over Niagara Falls. We were flying at 28,000 feet. It was a large aircraft but there were only about fifteen or twenty passengers. The captain came over and said, "If you've never seen Niagara from the air, you should go to the left of the aircraft and look down. It is a magnificent sight." I went to the left of the aircraft. The captain dipped the wings, and even at a distance of roughly ten miles, watching those three million gallons of water per minute fall and watching the spray come up thousands of feet, I got a feeling of the awesome power of Niagara. But for thousands of years, trillions of tons of water fell, hit the rocks, and dissipated in the distance below, utilizing only a minute fraction of the incredible power potential that was there.

Then one day a man came along and asked a question: "I wonder what would happen if I were to put a wheel under this falling water and catch part of it? Could we generate hydroelectricity?" To ask the question is to take the action, and that's exactly what they did. Since then, people have been able to build homes, schools, and factories. They've paved highways. They've built hospitals. They've raised the standard of living. They've healed the sick. They've raised crops. They've done it all because one day a man came along who had a plan.

What about you? Have you got a plan? Or will you go to work tomorrow because that's what you did yesterday?

Many years ago, Jean-Henri Fabre, the great French naturalist, conducted a series of experiments with some processionary caterpillars. They're so named because they follow one another in a procession. He lined them up around a flowerpot until they formed a never-ending circle. He watched them go around for a couple of hours. Then he became intrigued and said, "I wonder how long they'll keep it up."

The next day the caterpillars were still at it, so Fabre put some pine needles—the food of the processionary caterpillar—alongside the flowerpot. The next day they were still at it, and the next, and the next. For seven full days and nights they went round and round until they dropped dead from starvation and exhaustion, with an abundance of their favorite food less than three inches away. They starved to death because they confused activity with accomplishment.

We see that everywhere in life, don't we? People are busy, busy, busy, and they go, go, go, but they never get the job done because they have no plan of action. They'll go to work tomorrow because that's what they did yesterday.

Ten years after graduation, over 80 percent of the college graduates in America are earning their living in a field entirely different from the one they majored in while they were in college.

You've got to have goals. Imagine Sir Edmund Hillary, the first man to scale Mount Everest, climbing down from that mountain. A reporter comes up to him and says, "Tell me, Sir Edmund, how did you climb the tallest mountain in the whole world?" Do you for one moment think that he replied, "Well, I was just out walking around"?

Imagine the chairman of the board at General Motors. Somebody comes to him and asks, "How did you get to be chairman of the board for General Motors?" And he says, "I just showed up for work, and they started to promote me. And the first thing you know, here I am, chairman of the board of General Motors." Now we know that's ridiculous.

I find that goal setters, almost without exception, are around other goal setters. You become part of what you are around. The Bible says, "Be not deceived: evil communications corrupt good manners" (1 Corinthians 15:33). But the beautiful thing is that when you get into the right environment, you can change that over into the positive.

One of the most amazing stories I've ever read involves the late Shinichi Suzuki, a Japanese scientist who taught music to children starting when they were six weeks old. He would take a cassette player and put it beside the crib. The baby would listen to the beautiful music for a month; the next month, he would play another tune; the next month, another tune. For two solid years, this is what happened to that baby.

Then he would give the baby a miniature violin, about one-fifth regular size, and that child began to feel the instrument. At about two and a half, the mother of the child started taking violin lessons, with the child observing. When the child was about three years old, the child started taking the lessons. By the time it was five, it was playing beautiful music.

Suzuki once held a concert with over fifteen hundred Japanese children, with an average age of less than eight. They were not playing "Twinkle, Twinkle, Little Star." They were playing Chopin and Beethoven and Vivaldi—the classics. According to Suzuki, virtually none of these Japanese children had any "natural musical ability." It was a learned skill.

You can take your beautiful children, and you can feed them optimism, character, faith, truth, free enterprise, and responsibility. You can teach the good stuff just as surely as you can teach anything else. That's what excites me about life.

Speaking of goals, I don't think I was ever more impressed than I was when I read some statistics from the Korean War. During this war, for the first time in the history of our country, we did not have a single American prisoner of war who attempted to escape from minimum security prison camps. When the North Koreans captured our GIs, they went through a simple process of asking them some questions. Using the answers, they put the GIs either in minimum security or in maximum security prisons. From the maximum security prisons, sixty-nine men escaped. In minimum security, where conditions were relatively good, the death rate was three hundred times higher than it was in maximum security, where the conditions were intolerable. The prisoners in minimum security, with absolutely nothing wrong with them, lay down, pulled their blankets up over their heads, and died.

The North Koreans had a simple process. They asked the prisoners these questions: Are you excited about going back home? Do you love your wife? What is your relationship with your God? What do you think about America and the opportunities it has to offer? If a man loved his God, his wife, and his country and wanted to get back and build his life, they put him in maximum security. They knew he had a reason to get out and go back home. If he had no goals, if he did not have a religious conviction, if he did not love his country or his family, they put them in a minimum security camp, because they knew that there was a man who had no drive and no goals. He wasn't going to go anywhere.

In our country, we've been conditioned to believe that you've got to make a choice: you cannot build a magnificent career in the world of business and also build a beautiful family. At one point, *Esquire* magazine did a study of 179 of the top business executives in America; I'm talking about the presidents and the chairmen of the boards of major companies. They discovered that 95 percent of these men were still married to their first wives. They discovered that 139 of the 179 had been married to those ladies for over a quarter of a century.

How can you succeed both in business and with a family? The explanation was simple: the same qualities that make for good husbands and fathers also make for good administrators and executives. People who really care. People who are interested in having other people achieve their objectives. People who are communicators. People who are doing things because they really have some objectives in life.

People say, "Ziglar, how did you get sold on that idea about having goals?" I don't know if the name Howard Hill rings a bell with you or not. Howard Hill was a good Alabama boy who entered 286 archery tournaments and won first place 286 times. As a youngster, I saw newsreels of Howard Hill in archery tournaments where from fifty feet away, he would hit the bull's-eye perfectly in the center. Then he would take his next arrow and split the first one. An incredible demonstration of skill.

Even though I am not a professional archer, I am an instructor par excellence. I could spend twenty minutes with you and at the end of that time, I could have you hitting the bull's-eye more consistently than Howard Hill. Provided, of course, we had first blindfolded Howard Hill and turned him around a couple of times so he would not know which direction he was facing.

You may think, "That's the craziest thing I've ever heard in my life. How in the world could a man possibly hit a target he could not see?"

It's a good question. Here's one that I think is equally good. How can you hit a target you don't even have?

You may have some idea of where you're going to be someday. But until you start committing that to paper, until you list the obstacles that stand in your way, until you create a time limit, until you identify what you've got to learn, and until you start identifying the people, groups, organizations you need to work with, it's going to remain just a dream. That's all it's going to be.

In the end, you've got to have dreams. Scientists have studied the human brain a great deal. They have sophisticated machines where they can tell precisely when you go to sleep and start dreaming.

Scientists did a study, a very thorough one, on a large number of subjects. When they went to sleep and started to dream, the researchers would wake them up. Then they let them go back to sleep, but when they started to dream, the researchers would wake them up again.

After twenty-four hours of no dreams, the subjects were highly nervous, very agitated, very fidgety, and very difficult to get along with. After forty-eight hours of no dreams, they actually started seeing things coming out of the wall. At the end of seventy-two hours, they were close to real mental difficulty.

Finally, the researchers let the subjects go to sleep and dream. When they had finally gotten their quota of dreaming and they awakened, they were 99 percent back to normal, and one more night of sleep took care of the rest.

I believe that the dreams you dream when you're wide awake are equally important. You've got to have the vision.

Along about now, you might be saying, "OK, Ziglar, doggone, you've got me sold on those goals. Now how in the world am I going to identify those goals? What can I do about taking the necessary steps to get there?"

Think right now. Would you like to have a drink of water? Do you think it would be kind of nice if you had a drink right now?

Now this substance is colorless, odorless, and tasteless, but because of the conditioning process you've been in all of your life, you've probably started thinking, "Boy, I'd like to have a drink of water."

The intriguing fact is this: They tell us on television that they can sell millions of dollars' worth of merchandise subliminally with a thirty-two-second commercial. But then they say, "Don't worry about two hours of raw sex and pure violence, because after all, what possible harm could it do?"

The third reason most people don't have goals has to do with a poor self-image. They don't think they deserve to have a beautiful home. They don't think they deserve good kids or a magnificent car or a great bank account. They don't think they deserve to win. Psychologist Dr. Joyce Brothers says that the way you look, the way you dress, your moral conduct, your job, the profession you're in, the mate you select are determined by the way you see yourself. As I've already mentioned, Dr. David McClelland spent twenty-five years at Harvard University studying the subject, and he came to the inescapable conclusion that before you can improve your performance, you must improve or change the way you see yourself. I can tell you that in all the time I've dealt with the drug problem, I have never seen a youngster strung out on drugs who did not have a poor self-image.

I believe that one of the most damaging things that have ever happened in our country has been the teaching of the concept that we're animalistic in origin. I believe when you tell a little guy or a little girl that they are animalistic in origin, instead of telling them that they were created in God's own image, it makes a difference in the way they see themselves. I believe that horoscopes are similarly destructive, teaching that the day you were born has something to do with your moral conduct, your drive, your energy, and your ambition. I believe that pornography is even worse.

As I travel around the country, I read a lot of newspapers. Out of curiosity, I picked up a summation of the weekly soap operas. Just to give you an idea of how much damage is passed out in one week, I'm going to quote one. I want to give you an idea of what those people are doing:

Gus made a deathbed confession that he had killed his own daughter, Denise, because she planned to kill Miles and commit suicide. Before April heard that she had been cleared, she escaped prison. Miles and Nikolai argued when she admitted she had peeped at Wade's videotape before destroying it. Winter asked Margo for a job. April made her way to the house that she considers the source of her psychic power.

In these few lines, we've talked about confession, death, an argument, suspense, murder, suicide, conspiracy, a prison escape, robbery, vandalism, and witchcraft, not to mention unemployment. Now life is not that tough. But if you see that every day, can't you imagine the destructive impact it has?

At this point, I want to tell you my own story. I want to do that because many times when people hear me, they think, "I'll bet that guy was always that way." Nothing could be further from the truth.

I don't believe there's a man or woman whose shoes I have not already walked in. I don't believe anybody has ever been any broker than I've been or any more scared or than I've been or any more frustrated than I've been or who has had more doubts about tomorrow than I've had.

I'm one of twelve children. My dad died in 1932, when I was five years old. We lived in a small town, Yazoo City, Mississippi. I was milking the cows before I was eight years old. (Anybody who thinks cows give milk has never milked a cow.) I was selling vegetables on the streets of that little Mississippi town by the time I was eight years old. Before I entered the fifth grade, I went to work in a grocery store. I was a teller. Don't get hung up on the title: that just meant that I told people to move while I swept. I bought every set of clothing I've ever owned since before I was ten years old.

I was a little bitty guy. One of the signs of a poor self-image is an individual who's always arguing and fighting with people. I fought everybody that moved. I never discriminated; it made no difference to me whether they were black or white or tall or short or fat or slim or—I'm embarrassed to say it—whether they were littler or bigger than I was. If we couldn't settle the argument in about ten seconds, I reared back and flat out busted them. A Mexican boy broke me of that habit. I've never been as glad to see a schoolteacher in my life as I was when she finally got there and broke it up.

I weighed less than 120 pounds, fully dressed, as a senior in high school. I never dated a girl till after I was seventeen years old, and that was a blind date somebody else got for me. I had an image of myself of a little guy from a little town who would struggle all his life.

To this day, I can well remember that we used to sit out on the front porch of our home and argue about what was the best, the Ford or the Chevrolet. Mr. Fred Shirley, the rural mail carrier, had a Chevrolet. Dr. Tom Reyner, the doctor in the town, who lived a block from us, drove a Ford. We always used to argue about which one we were going to get.

I had a dream as a child. Mr. Shirley traded in that little Chevrolet coupe every year. It cost about $150 a year to trade those cars in at that time, but it might as well have been $150,000 for most of us. I dreamed that when I became a man, I was going to be at that Chevrolet dealership, and when Mr. Shirley traded his car in, I was going to be able to buy his used Chevrolet coupe. My idea of a dream vacation was to go as far as that little car would take me in a week and come back in two weeks. When I came back, I saw myself owning my own little meat market.

I never saw myself living in the slums, but I saw myself on the outskirts of town. I always had an acre of ground in mind, and I was going to have a big garden, because when I was on the downside of life, I still saw myself having to raise that little garden and sell the vegetables for the additional income.

When World War II came along, I got in on the tail end of it. I never went anywhere or did anything. The war was winding down. I met that redhead of mine, my wife, during that period. We got married not long after I was discharged. We would go to the University of South Carolina, selling sandwiches at the dormitories at night. Business was good in the winter months; it didn't exist in the summer months.

My wife saw an ad in the paper where they wanted a $10,000 a year salesman. We thought it was providential that they wanted a $10,000 salesman, because we wanted the $10,000. So I went down and applied for the job: it was selling cookware on a door-to-door basis on commission. I had to buy my own samples, but they didn't think I could sell, so it took me over two months to get the job.

For the next two and a half years, all I did was prove they'd been right. Don't misunderstand: that didn't mean I didn't sell a lot, because I did. I sold my furniture, sold my car. I've walked down the grocery line and miscalculated and had to put a loaf of bread back.

When my own daughter was born, the hospital bill was $64. The problem was, I didn't have the $64. I had to get out and sell two sets of cookware in order to get my own daughter out of the hospital.

Money almost always seemed to be out of our reach. Once I got a little bit ahead—$50: two $20 bills and a $10 bill; they were laid bottom side up in one of my drawers. I'd put them there, thinking someday I'd have a rainy day, and I'd forgotten about them. A few months later, I was rummaging around and there that $50 was. I'd never seen that much money in my life. I thought it was the most beautiful sight I've ever seen.

You might ask why I didn't try to get another job. I'd gone so deeply in debt that I could not find another one that would pay me enough. I had to sell my way out, and I knew it, but there were discouraging times. For two and a half years, it was doubt. Many nights I'd go to bed and say, "Tomorrow I'll get out there and get them." But when you've got a poor self-image, when you've rejected yourself, you will procrastinate.

Then one day my world changed. I did a 180-degree turn. I'd gone up to Charlotte, North Carolina, spent a day in a training school, and didn't learn a thing.

I'd driven back that night, I'd had a cookware demonstration, and got in about 11:30. We lived in a little three-room apartment above a grocery store, and the baby kept us up most of the rest of the night. At 5:30 the next morning, the alarm clock—today, it's an opportunity clock, but in those days, it was an alarm clock—sounded. Force of habit rolled me out of bed. I cracked the venetian blinds, and snow was coming down. I was driving a Crosley automobile without a heater.

So I did what any intelligent human being would do. That's right: I got back in bed. But as I lay down, the words of my mother came back to me, the conditioning I'd gone through. She said, "Son if you're in something, get in, and if you're not in it, get out.

When you're hired out to a man, you're hired out to do everything he pays you to do. If in good conscience you cannot do that, then you'd better get another job, because you'll never succeed in that one. You're not being fair to him, and you're not being fair to you."

I rolled out of bed and made a cold trip to Charlotte, North Carolina. When the meeting was over, Mr. P. C. Merrell, the man who was conducting it that day, called me aside. He said, "Zig, I'd like to talk with you for a moment after everyone else has gone."

I cannot begin to tell you what it meant to me that Mr. P. C. Merrell, who was my hero, wanted to talk with me. It did wonders for my image that he just wanted to say hello to me.

When he got me aside, he said, "Zig, I have watched you for the last two and a half years, and I've never seen such a waste."

Now that'll get your attention. I looked at him and said, "Mr. Merrell, what do you mean?"

"Zig, I'm convinced that you could be a great one. I'm convinced that you could go all the way to the top. I'm convinced that you could become a national champion. Maybe someday you could even become an executive in this company, if you just believed in yourself and went to work on a regular schedule."

I'd been told for the last two-and-a-half years that I ought to go to work on a regular schedule. But you see, when you've got a poor self-image, you rationalize: why should I get out there today when nothing good is going to happen to me anyhow? You tell a student, "You ought to study your lesson so you'll get ahead in life." If that student has a poor self-image, they're going to think, "Why should I study? Nothing good is ever going to happen to me, because I don't deserve it." You tell a youngster with a poor self-image, "You ought to obey the law," and many times, they will think, "Why should I obey the law? The deck's already stacked. Nothing good is ever going to happen to me. Why shouldn't I go ahead and have some fun?"

But when Mr. Merrell said to me, "You could be a great one," I respected his integrity. It never occurred to me that he was trying to jack me up so that I would sell more cookware and make him look good. He said, "You could be a national champion," and I believed him.

I had a demonstration that night. Today I know it was not a coincidence that I did. There were three couples there. I don't know if they were good prospects, bad prospects, or average prospects. All I knew is that I knew that when they walked in, they were going to buy the cookware. I sold all three.

Before the year was over, I was the number two salesman in America, out of seven thousand. I had swapped that Crosley, which I had difficulty paying for, for a nice car, which I easily paid for. I had the best promotion that company had. The next year, as far as I've been able to find out, I was the company's highest paid manager in the United States. Three years later, I became the youngest divisional supervisor in the sixty-six-year history of that company and set some records which stand until this day.

If I were to sum it all up, I would say that the only thing that changed about me was the way I saw myself. Today I never speak, whether it's for a mammoth organization, for a thousand, or for a dozen, until I first of all have gotten on my knees and asked God to make me a P. C. Merrell in your life.

I would love to be able to spend just a moment with every human being who reads one of my books, or hears one of my audios, or to whom I ever speak in an audience, because if I had that one moment, I would look you right in the eye. I'd ask God to let me see your heart, and I would tell you that you are designed for accomplishment. I would tell you that you're engineered for success. I would tell you that you're endowed with the seeds of greatness. I would tell you that God loves you and that he wants you to make it. I would remind you that over ten billion people have walked this earth, but there never has been, and there never will be, another one like you. You're rare, you're different, you're special, you're somebody.

God created you in his own image, and because he created you, he believes in you. But he leaves the deciding vote entirely up to you. So I invite you to step into the polling booth of your own mind. Visualize reaching up, grabbing the curtains, and pulling them shut, because this is a private affair. Then

I want you to reach up and grab the lever that has your name on it, and I want you to pull that lever vigorously down and say, "I vote for me." When you pull the lever down and vote for you, all you've got to do is look and you'll see that God has already voted for you. With those two votes, you can win any election or any contest you will ever enter in your life. Vote for you, believe in you, and you can do it.

FIVE

Setting Goals

Now that we've established that you need to set goals, the next question comes up: how do you set them? I've often heard somebody say, "Zig, you got my soul alive, and my image is better. I believe I deserve the good life. I recognize the necessity of those goals. The fear has been removed, it's been established that yes, I can do something with my life, but I just don't know how. Can you enlighten me?"

If that's been your loser's limp up until now and you want to continue to use it as a loser's limp, I urge you to put this book down right now, because I'm going to pull that rug out from under you forever.

Once I was doing a session down in San Antonio. A little lady came up to me at the break and asked, "Can you have more than one goal?"

My response to her was, "If you only have one goal, you're going to end up a warped individual."

The reason is very simple: life is far more complex than that. We are physical, we are mental, and we are spiritual. If we don't deal with all three of those things, we are not going to have balanced success in our life. I'm primarily going to be talking about physical, financial, and family goals, but I want to also emphasize that you need to throw in social goals, spiritual goals, career goals, and many other kinds. They are all tied together, but you must have more than one goal.

Let me give you an analogy. If someone were to invite me to come and give a lecture on bodybuilding and weight lifting in two years, I honestly believe that in that period, I could spend enough time lifting weights and studying physiology to become an authority on those subjects. I believe I would be able to peel down my shorts and show you my muscles. I really do.

But if I did, it would be at the sacrifice of my career. My finances would suffer, my spiritual life would suffer, my relationship with that redhead would suffer. I would, in short, sacrifice entirely too much.

You've got to live a balanced life. If I make millions and end up with ulcers, I don't consider that to be a successful life. If I go all the way to the top of my profession but alienate my wife and my children along the way, I don't believe I'm successful. I believe that health, wealth, and happiness are the natural result of building on the right foundation and living a balanced life.

As I've said, I am an optimist. I believe all of these things are available if we do certain things and take certain steps, so let's look at the goals and the way they're set.

When I started writing *See You at the Top*, the first thing I wrote down was, "You can go where you want to go, you can do what you want to do, you can be the way you want to be." As I read those words, I said to myself, "Ziglar, that's pretty good."

I hasten to add that it is perfectly all right to talk to yourself. Once I was on a program with psychologist Dr. Joyce Brothers, who observed—and it has now been scientifically established—that people who talk to themselves are above average in intelligence. I believe it's perfectly all right even to answer yourself. But if you ever catch yourself saying, "Huh?" you've got a problem.

When I wrote, "You could be the way you want to be," I noticed I was holding the page way out, because between me and the book was a forty-one-inch waistline and 202 pounds of Ziglar. It occurred to me that one day I'd bump into a slender dude, and I could visualize him saying, "Ziglar, you believe all that stuff you write?"

I was going to say, "Man, yeah."

Then I could visualize that guy looking at me really carefully and saying, "Do you believe it all?"

"Of course I do."

Then I could visualize him poking his finger into that forty-one-inch waistline and saying, "Ziglar, do you believe it?"

I would have said, "Well, you know, we authors do take a little literary license every once in a while."

"Ziglar, is that your fancy way of saying you lied about it?"

"Now, hold on, friend, don't call me a liar; people don't like liars."

"Well, you're at least a hypocrite."

I knew that either I had to do something about those words in that book or I had to do something about me. The straw that broke the camel's back was that redhead telling me, "Hold your stomach in," when I already was.

I decided to go down to the clinic of Dr. Kenneth Cooper, the man who wrote the book *Aerobics*. When you see people jogging around, you can rest assured that either directly or indirectly, he has influenced their life.

I went down for the six-hour examination. The first thing they did was took two quarts of my blood. Or it looked like two quarts. I'll tell you, they filled so many vials, I thought they were opening a branch of the blood bank right there.

Then they dunked me in a tank of water to determine my percentage of body fat. When I got through, they told me I was 23.1 percent pure lard. Then they put me on a treadmill, where I walked and I walked and I walked. The longer you can walk, the better your physical condition. The worst possible physical condition was "horrible." I determined as I watched those dials that I was going to get out of horrible into just awful, and I made it by four seconds.

When it was all over, Dr. Martin, a skinny, young doctor—highly motivated, very enthusiastic, ran in the Boston Marathon—called me in with a big grin on his face. He said, "Mr. Ziglar, I ran the figures through the computer. We've done a complete analysis, we know they're absolutely accurate, and you're going to be delighted to know that you, sir, are not overweight." However, he said, "According to the computer, you're exactly five and a half inches too short."

"Well, doc, that's pretty bad, ain't it?"

"Actually, you're in remarkably good physical condition for a sixty-six-year-old."

"Doc, I'm forty-six."

"You're in awful shape. As a matter of fact, if you were a building, I'd condemn you."

"Well, doc, what can I do?"

He whipped out sheet of papers thicker than my book and started telling me what I could do. By the time I got through, I was like the little boy who asks his daddy questions. Dad says, "Son, why don't you just ask your mother?" The little boy says, "Dad, I really don't want to know that much about it."

When I got home, the redhead said, "I suppose you're going to be out running all over the neighborhood."

"Yes, I am."

"Well, if I'm going to have a forty-six-year-old fat boy running all over the place, I'm going to get you looking as good as I can."

So she went down to the store and bought me some fancy running shirts and shorts, and I'd gotten the shoes the doctor recommended. There were some that were really ugly.

I came across an advertisement for Jockey shorts in a magazine. If you look at those ads, you'll find out in a hurry that they don't put Jockey shorts on fat boys. So I cut out the picture, hung it up in my bathroom mirror, and said, "Now there's my hero; that's the way I'm going to be."

The next morning, that opportunity clock sounded off bright and early. I rolled out of bed, put that fancy running outfit on, went out the front door, and ran a block all by myself. I woke the family up and said, "Guess what dad has done?"

I did better the next day: around a block and a mailbox. The next day, it was a block and two mailboxes, then a block and three, a block and four, a block and five. One day, I ran half a mile, then a mile, then two miles. I started doing sit-ups: only eight the first day, then ten, then twenty, then fifty, then a hundred, then two hundred. I started doing push-ups: six on the first day, then eight and ten, then twenty, then forty. Then I would do the GI push-up, meaning a push-up where I slap my hands while I'm in the air. The weight started coming down from 202 to 165, the waistline from 41 to 34.

A lot of people said, "Yeah, but I bet you were dieting religiously all of that time too." Well, that answer is partially right, because I did quit eating in church.

I will digress just for a moment and say that if you're serious about losing weight, I will give you four very simple suggestions that will have a dramatic impact on your weight loss.

Number one, and by far the most important is this: stay away from cottage cheese, which is the most fattening food in existence. I understand I have no scientific evidence to support this, but I'm totally certain that I'm right, because in over three million miles of traveling over the years, I have noticed that nobody eats that stuff but fat folks, so stay away from it.

Number two: get a thorough examination from your skinny doctor. If he's not skinny, get another doctor, because his credibility is going to suffer. A doctor sitting there with his stomach hanging over his belt, telling you about the glories of being slender, and you're thinking, "Doc, if it's good for me, how come it ain't good for you too?"

Number three: if a doctor attempts to give you a prescription to help you lose the weight, don't walk out on him, run out. You did not gain the weight by taking pills, and you are not going to lose the weight by taking pills. It's just that simple. Again according to Dr. Joyce Brothers, your doctor has got something like thirty times a chance of becoming a drug addict than you do. The reason is availability. Got a headache? Take a pill. Can't get started in the morning? Take a pill. Can't unwind? Take a pill. Can't sleep? Take a pill. Can't relax? Take a pill—until the pill becomes the problem.

Number four: if you're really serious about losing weight and your doctor is a negative doctor, get another one. What's a negative doctor? A doctor who says you can't eat this and can't eat that. In other words, you can't eat anything you like. That's why a lot of people never go to the doctor, because they know he's going to say, "Don't, don't, don't." In most cases, they're Doctor Don'ts.

I loved Dr. Martin, because he was so positive. He looked at me and said, "Mr. Ziglar, you're going to be delighted to know that you can eat anything you want. Here's a list of what you're going to want."

People are always asking me, "Zig, what can't you eat?" I have no earthly idea of what I can't eat. I'm not going to fill my mind with a bunch of stuff I can't have anyhow. If you ask me what I *can* eat, I'll tell you roast beef, steak, chicken, fish, fruits, salads, and vegetables. I can eat all of those good things; why should I even think about the things I cannot have?

I tell this story about losing weight because it involves every single principle of goal setting and goal reaching.

Number one, and this is the most critical area, the goal was mine. My redhead was delighted when I decided to lose the weight, but it was not her idea. My doctor gave me the best way to do it, but it was not his idea either.

You've got a lot of lousy doctors, lawyers, preachers, and other professionals out there because they're doing, not what they wanted to do, but what their mothers or daddies or grandparents or professors told them: "You ought to do this with your life." They said, "Well, I don't have anything else to do. OK, I'll do it." Many people go to work for XYZ Company for no other reason than that a friend of theirs said, "Man, it's a good company. We've got a good retirement plan and all those good things. Come on down." Twenty years later, they're still going to work every day at something they never really selected for themselves.

To get back to diets, the reason most of them do not work is twofold. Number one, the person's image is not in its proper place. They do not think they deserve to be slender. They don't think they deserve to be healthy, so they gorge themselves.

The second reason is that the person never actually had weight loss as a goal. The husband said, "You've got to lose that weight"; the wife said, "You've got to lose that weight"; the doctor said, "You've got to lose that weight." Society itself has decreed that slender is healthy; therefore you've got to lose the weight. You go to the magazine rack right now, and I guarantee you, you'll find a brand-new diet on the cover of at least three different magazines. Neighborhood tested, doctor approved, lose twenty-nine pounds in sixteen days; slow, easy, simple, painless—all of those good things. All of those diets will work or none of them will work, depending on whether you make it yours or not.

Many times the poor victim hears everybody say, "You've got to lose that weight." So he does it for three days, till some dirty dog rolls the pastry cart by. Then will meets imagination, and when will bumps up against imagination, will's going to get whupped a hundred times out of a hundred.

Then there's the second thing: when I went to the doctor, I did so to find out where I was. If you want to build a better relationship with your children, you'd better find out where you are right now. How are you doing? According to the National PTA, the average parents spend seven and a half minutes a week in direct communication with their kids. I'm not talking about while they're having a meal or watching television. I mean when it's just the parent and the child, and they're talking about life and love and their future.

The third thing about my weight loss goal was that it was a big goal. We need some big goals in our lives, because they force us to reach inside and utilize the enormous potential there. The kite rises only against the wind. Your muscles develop only when there is resistance. You never acquire sales skills if everybody you talk to instantly buys what you are selling. The tough prospects are the best teachers of them all.

Gentleman Jim Corbett, the late heavyweight champion of the world, was doing his roadwork one morning when he ran past a fisherman who was having a banner day. He was pulling in fish after fish after fish, but Corbett noticed that the fisherman kept the little ones and threw the big ones back. Curiosity got the better of Corbett. He ran over to the fisherman and said, "I don't understand: you're keeping the little ones and throwing the big ones back. Why are you doing it?"

The fisherman sadly shook his head and said, "Don't think I don't hate to do it. I really do. But I don't have any choice, because all I've got is a small frying pan."

Before you laugh, let me warn you: he's talking about you and me. Many times when we get a big dream or a big idea, another thought follows right behind it, and we say, "Oh, no, Lord. Don't give me such a big one. All I've got is a small frying pan." Poor little me. My image won't let me dream the big dream."

Obviously not all goals have to be big goals. You can take a youngster, and you'll be astonished at what it does for his self-image if he makes up his bed and straightens his room every morning, because that's a task he completes.

You build a child's self-images by requiring him to cut the grass. Why? Because it's high and over-grown with weeds. Two hours later, it's nice and smooth, and he can look back and say, "This I have done, and I like what I've done; therefore, I like *me* better because I like what I've done."

Every time you complete any task, whether it's finishing a book or conducting a meeting under difficult circumstances, you like *you* a little bit better, and that enables you to reach a little higher for those goals.

In order for a goal to be effective, it must effect change. It's got to make a difference in your life. I've got old pictures and movies from when I weighed over two hundred pounds. When I really want to get a laugh, I look at one of them for a few minutes. And I walk out pulling in my stomach and really feeling good.

The fourth thing about that goal—and again, this is important—is that it was very specific. Losing thirty-seven pounds is very specific. You can take the hottest day the world has ever seen, take the most powerful magnifying glass you can buy, and hold it over a pile of newspaper clippings. You'll never start a fire if you keep the glass moving, but the minute you hold the glass still and harness the power of the sun through the glass, boom! You've got a fire.

The bird hunter who shoots to the flock comes home empty-handed. The hunter who says, "I'll get that one"—he's the one who comes back with the birds in the bag. That's what I'm talking about. You've got to zero in on exactly what you want.

There's no way it could be any more specific than I just said: I needed to lose exactly thirty-seven pounds. You can dream about having a family reunion, or you can say, I'm going to have 1,738 people in the ballroom of the Hilton Hotel in Denver on August 22. Now you're being specific. Now you can zero in on the things you really want.

You've also got to be aware of accomplishment feedback. When I started losing weight and came in under two hundred, I felt good all over. When I came under 190, that was a major accomplishment. I said, "Man, don't I ever feel good!"

If you are on a weight loss program, I suggest that every time you reach one of your objectives—like a ten-pound weight loss—you treat yourself to something nice. Buy a new purse, a new pair of shoes, a new shirt or sports coat. As you do, you are saying to yourself, "This is my reward for having reached an objective." Accomplishment feedback gives you the confidence that you're going to be able to go on and do something else.

If you don't have any long-range goals, a short-range goal becomes the entire oceanfront. But if you do have long-range goals, you understand that that is simply a pebble on the beach. People who have long-range goals almost never become negative, because they're looking beyond today. They know that today is another experience preparing them for a bigger, brighter, better tomorrow. The beauty about long-range goals is that you go as far as you can see. When you get there, you're going to be able to see further. And if you have difficulties along the way (which you will), you're not destroyed.

When I was writing my book *See You at the Top*, I figured that it was going to take me ten months. I decided to tie a couple of goals together.

When I was finished, I sent the manuscript off to three major publishers. I knew that in short order, I would have a check for at least $100,000 in advance royalties. I could visualize them standing in line, saying, "Oh, Mr. Ziglar, please let us publish this magnificent creation of yours, which is going to sell millions of copies."

I could visualize that happening to me; I knew it would. As a matter of fact, I met the postman every day for the next two weeks, and the letters started coming back from all three of them. They beat around the bush for three paragraphs. In the fourth paragraph, they said something like, "Under the present circumstances, market conditions being what they are, we feel that the public interest and confidence on a book of this nature is not something that is conducive to us making a sustained effort to publicize it and bring it into the view of the American public." Translated, that means, "We don't think it's going to sell."

I could not conceive of three supposedly intelligent people arriving at such an idiotic decision.

I knew beyond any reasonable doubt that the book would sell for a very simple reason: I write exactly the way I talk. People were responding to the way I was talking; therefore I knew they would respond to the book.

At that point, I had to make a decision. It's one thing for me to ask you to put your money in my book. It's an entirely different thing for *me* to put my money in my book. Was I willing to reach into my pocket, bring out the money, and say, "Yes, I believe in the book; therefore print it?"

I decided that I was willing to make the commitment. A friend of mine said, "Zig, if you sell 20,000 copies, you've got a bestseller." I don't ever like to play things too carefully or closely, so I decided that instead of 20,000 copies, I would publish 25,000 copies. Now I don't know what you know about publishing books, but I can tell you one thing: when you publish 25,000 copies, the first one costs more than the next 24,999. I'm talking about a bunch of money.

The first chapter I wrote was on goals. I wrote that I weighed 165 pounds and that I had a 34-inch waistline. The day I wrote those words, I weighed 202 pounds and had a 41-inch waistline. Now can you imagine me with 25,000 copies of this book in the warehouse, saying I weighed 165, and I come waddling out on stage at 202?

Credibility is important, not as a moral issue but as a practical issue. Because the day comes when we need to depend on other people. If they've been unable to depend on us, if our word is of no value, then why should they stick their necks out again for us?

I knew that if I did not deliver on my goal as set down in my book, my credibility was going to be destroyed. I projected that it would take me 10 months to write the book. I needed to lose 37 pounds. I looked at the 37 pounds divided by 10, and it came out to 3.7 pounds a month. I got excited, because I knew that I could lose that amount fast— not even a pound a week. As a matter of fact, I was so confident that I could lose those pounds in a month that I didn't even bother to get started for the first 28 days.

Do you know anybody like that? Do you know anybody who says, "I'm really anxious to get started, but it's almost time for the kids to get out of school. I'll wait till then, and I'll have more time, then I'll really get busy." As soon as the kids get out of school, they say, "I didn't realize it, but now these kids are involved in so many things. I've got to take them somewhere every day, so I might as well wait till they go back to school; then I'll really get out there and build a business."

When the kids get back in school, they say, "For the first time in eleven years, old Central has finally got a winning football team. You've got to support the kids in these things. We're going to support the football team. Wait until after football season is over, and then I'll really go." Football season ends, and they say, "Thanksgiving, Christmas, and New Year's are coming, and people don't want to be bothered this time of year. When the holidays are behind us, I'll have a free mind, and I'll get out there and tear them up."

As soon as the holiday season is over, they say, "Isn't this the most peculiar weather you have ever seen in your life? I've never seen weather like this. Wait till it clears up. You're thinking that I'm losing interest, but that's not it. See, I'm a deliberate type of individual. I line everything up in order: one, two, three, four. When I have them all lined up, I get it all done in a systematic way."

When the weather clears, these people say, "It's Easter, and that's family time." As soon as that's over, they say, "At long last, we've got some good weather, and I haven't been fishing or hit a golf ball in so long. You can't work all the time. You've got to have some recreation." After that, they say, "It's almost time for the kids to get out of school." That's where we came in, is it not?

When I was growing up in Yazoo City, we lived next door to some rich folks. I know they were rich for two reasons: number one, they had a cook; number two, the cook had something to cook.

Don't misunderstand: even though there was a depression on, we certainly had plenty to eat at my house. I know because when I passed my plate for seconds, they'd always tell me, "No, you've had plenty."

Anyway, I was over there for lunch one day, as I tried to be every day. The cook brought the biscuits out. No exaggeration: those biscuits were not as thick as my wristwatch. I looked at them and said, "What in the world happened to your biscuits?" The cook said, "I'll tell you about those biscuits. They squatted to rise, but they just got cooked in the squat"—meaning they were cooked before they rose.

Now who gets cooked in the squat? I'll tell you who. The people who wait for the kids to get out of school or the new models to come in. The people who wait till John gets on the day shift. The people who wait for the new governor or senator, or for other external conditions to change before they make an internal move. They're the ones who invariably end up getting cooked in the squat.

I'll say without batting an eyelash that I would rather have you invest ten minutes in your goals before you go to sleep tonight than tell me you're going to put in ten hours on them next week. The word is, *do it now.*

Let me go on about setting goals and what is really involved. I wrote down exactly what I want to lose, that is, thirty-seven pounds. I recognized there were some obstacles I had to overcome. I like bread and I love sweets; I snack a lot; I eat between meals; I've had all of those bad habits. I recognized that I needed some outside help; that's why I went to the doctor to get advice on how to do it. I read the books on running and talked with my family about the best way to do it. I set a precise time limit on how long it was going to take me to get there, and I acquired the knowledge from doctors and books. I outlined the steps and kept up with them, so I knew that I was going to get there. I had made the commitment.

SIX

How to Train Fleas

Many years ago, an international expedition attempted to climb the north wall of the Matterhorn, which at that time had never been done. A reporter went to one of the climbers and said, "What do you think about it? What are your chances?"

He said, "I'm going to give it everything I got."

The reporter went to another one and asked, "What do you think about your chances?"

"I'm going to give it all my bloody effort," he said.

The reporter went to still another man and asked, "What are your chances of climbing the north wall of the Matterhorn?"

This man looked at him dead center, and without any braggadocio, but with the confidence that comes with the knowledge that he had the skills and had done his homework, said, "I will climb the north wall of the Matterhorn."

That man was the one person who did it. He had made a commitment.

There is something else involved in achieving goals, and that is discipline. I've had many people come up to me and ask, "Ziglar, tell me the truth. Did you really enjoy getting up in the morning and doing all of that running?"

I'm going to tell you the truth: I hated it. That opportunity alarm would sound off, I'd reach over, and I'd shut it off. And I'd ask myself, "Ziglar, what's a forty-six-year-old fat boy like you doing running all over the neighborhood? Your buddies are soundly sleeping in bed. What are you trying to prove?"

Then I looked down at that forty-one-inch waist-line, which said, "Ziglar do you want to look like *you*, or do you want to look like the guy in the Jockey shorts?"

I didn't want to look like me, so I got out of bed, but that didn't necessarily mean I was going to be having fun. I said, "God, I said I'm going to do it. I'm going to do it even if it kills me."

You watch a motivational speaker long enough and you listen to him long enough, and before that rascal gets through, he's going to end up looking at you, giving an impassioned plea with pain on his face and a strain in his voice. He's going to say, "You've got to pay the price." That is undoubtedly the biggest bunch of baloney that has ever been foisted on an unsuspecting American public.

One day I was running on the campus of Portland State University in Portland, Oregon. It was a magnificent spring day, about seventy-eight degrees, at high noon. I had a seminar at 4:00 p.m. I looked around and noticed many of the students were laying out their blankets. Some were reading, some were studying, some snoozing, and here comes old Ziglar running by, with sweat dripping down my back and legs. That day, all of a sudden for the first time, it hit me like a ton of bricks that I no longer was paying the price; I was having the time of my life.

So when you tell me, "You've got to pay the price for good health," I'm going to tell you, "You've got the wrong guy. You don't pay the price for good health; you enjoy the price of good health." Tell me you've got to pay the price to raise beautiful, loving, disciplined children, and I'm going to say, "No way. You're going to thoroughly enjoy the price." Tell me you've got to pay the price for success, and I'm going to point to the failures in life. I've never known a happy failure.

I tell this story in all of its details because it involves discipline. Every morning for ten solid months at exactly 5:00 a.m.,—regardless of what time I went to bed—out of bed I rolled. Yes, it was tough many times, but I learned more about time utilization and discipline in those ten months than in all the rest of my life put together.

I'm probably the most time-conscious individual I know. My wife tells me I'm a workaholic, but she will also tell you that when I'm at home, I seldom if ever do anything but pay attention to her and my son and things around the house. When I'm on a trip, I can average two telephone calls while I'm waiting on my baggage to come down. If I'm tired after a seminar, I get aboard the airplane, and I'm asleep before it leaves the ground. When it hits cruising altitude, I start working. When we start our descent, I quit writing and start reading. Sometimes when I'm making my telephone calls, I have a book in front of me, and I can read a page while I'm waiting for the secretary to get the boss on the telephone.

You might tell yourself, "I don't ever want to get that involved," but I've been able to take several short vacation trips a year, because when I'm working, I am flat out getting after it.

Again it is a question of discipline. I'm amazed at the number of people who say to me, "I don't have time to do this or that," but when they analyze their time, they discover that they've invested several hours every week in watching television or reading trash. You need to discipline your mind and keep your eyes on what you want.

You train fleas by putting them in a jar and putting the top on the jar. The fleas will jump up and hit the top over and over hundreds of times, and all of a sudden, you will notice that even though they're continuing to jump, they are no longer hitting the top. Then you can take the top off, and those fleas will keep on jumping and jumping, but they cannot jump out. The reason is very simple: they have been conditioned to jump just so high. Once they've been conditioned to jump just so high, that's all there is, and there ain't no more.

Man is exactly the same way. We start out in life intending to climb the high mountain, to write the book, to break the record. Along the way, we stub our toes, we bump our heads, and we become what I call a SNIOP: a person who is Susceptible to the Negative Influence of Other People. We see him all the time.

The four-minute mile is the classic case. For years, people said, "I'm going to run the four-minute mile," and the doctor would look at them and say, "Man, your heart will come out of your body. You can't do it." The coach would say, "Who do you think you're kidding? Man alive, there ain't no way."

Then one day a runner named Roger Bannister came along, and he set his goal. He carefully charted the obstacles and set a time limit on it. He broke the program down into segments. He had the accomplishment feedback. He enlisted the aid of others to run with him and set the pace. And one day Roger Bannister broke the four-minute barrier, and the minute he broke it, athletes the world over said, "If he can, I can." Less than six weeks later, John Landy of Australia also broke the four-minute barrier. From that day until this, hundreds of people have run the mile in less than four minutes.

In one race, in Baton Rouge, Louisiana, eight guys ran a mile in less than four minutes in the same race, not because they got that much faster, but because they understood: it was not a physical impossibility; it was a mental barrier. Once the record has been broken, it is being broken all the time.

What's a winner? A winner is a person who is driven from within. A winner is an individual who is not influenced by the negative attitudes of others. A lot of people say, "He makes me so mad" or "She makes me so mad." No, they don't—not until you give them specific permission to come into your mind and tell you how to act and think and feel. A winner is not influenced by the SNIOP; they're driven from within. They make their own decisions. A winner understands that you can get everything in life you want if you just help enough other people get what they want. Winners don't tell other people where to get off; they show them how to get on. A winner, in other words, is that rare individual who does not try to see through people, but to see people through.

You've also got to have dreams. Decades ago, I dreamed that I would be going all over the world, doing what I'm doing. I made thousands of speeches in my mind before I ever got a dime for one of them.

What a tragedy that we could not record those speeches I made in my mind! I wish you could have just heard one of them. When I would come out with these incredibly magnificent words of wisdom, the audience would sit there in open-mouthed astonishment that a mortal man could utter such gems. In those speeches in my mind, my average standing ovation was in excess of eleven minutes. People just stood up and kept going on and on.

Every dream I've ever dreamed, with the exception of that eleven-minute standing ovation, has become a reality.

I want you to be very careful about what you dream. As you and your mind build an organization, as you build a home, as you build a business, you're going to be confronted with the incredible responsibilities that go along with it. Because as you dream those dreams, people are going to look at you and, in many cases, emulate you.

I never realized how true that was until I listened to a recording made by the late Charlie Calhoun that I had not heard in several years. As I listened, I realized that I was using some of the same voice inflections that I thought were so effective for him. I did not do it deliberately, but I instinctively picked up some of his mannerisms.

Furthermore, when you dream, you've got to see yourself in the home you want or standing in front of the organization you want to build. You've got to give your dream all of the vivid details, in all the shapes and sizes and colors.

Let me say this: the most important person that you ever deal with in your life is the first person you deal with every day. I spend as much time as I do talking about the family environment because if an individual has a good relationship at home, they are going to do better out in the world. The support of a mate is of critical importance.

If I gave a talk and everybody here comes to me and say, "Man alive, you are fantastic" and if my own family did not, the meeting would not have been nearly as successful as it otherwise would have been. Writer Raymond Hull expressed it beautifully when he said that the applause of a single human being is of great consequence. If it's the applause of the one you love the most, it has more meaning than all of the others put together.

So applaud your husbands and wives. Support each other, because when you do, you establish that attitude which is so critically important.

A good friend of mine, a medical doctor in Amarillo, Texas, said you could take a big glass, fill it full of the most deadly poison known to man, and drink it without harm—provided you diluted it with several million gallons of water. "Zig, I don't know how many millions of gallons it'll take," he said, "so I urge you not to try." But at least theoretically, you can dilute the poison down to the degree that it will not have a negative effect on you.

I believe the greatest poison in America today is negativism. I have identified some of these, but we cannot live in a sterile, isolated world. We're going to encounter some negativities, so I'm going to say to you that every day, the most important person in influencing your attitude is going to be the first one. The first person you meet has a bigger bearing on your attitude than the next five you will meet. That ought to be your mate.

Start every day with humor, optimism, hope, and enthusiasm. Get ready for what you're going to encounter out there. Build the right mental attitude. Feed your mind.

I also believe that if you change the way you answer the telephone, it can be tremendously beneficial. Many people pick up the telephone as if it were an intrusion; they say, "Yeah?" or "What do you want?" In my office, our receptionist says, "Good morning" (and you *know* it's a good morning), and then she makes a motivational speech. It's not as long as the ones I make, but she says, "It's a great day." A lot of time people ask, "Zig, is it always a great day?" Certainly. It's always a great day, and if you don't believe me, you just missed one. Then she identifies the name of the company.

When I'm at home, I pick the telephone up saying, "And a good morning to you." Now I'll be the first to admit sometimes there's a long pause. Then I zing them another one: "If you don't speak up, I'm going to hang up."

If they say, "Who is this?" I'll say, "Whoever you want. Who do you want?"

"Man, you sure do feel good today."

I say, "Yes, I'd made a decision many years ago that I was going to feel good today." It's a matter of choice.

On other days, I'll pick up the telephone and say, "Howdy. Howdy. Howdy." People ask, "Do you always feel that good?" I say, "No, but I always want to feel that good, and the only way I'm going to feel that good is to act like I already did feel that good."

Logic will not change an emotion, but action will, and I'm taking the action. People say, "What are the benefits?" The benefits are enormous. Number one, it makes me feel better, and number two, it makes the individual at the other end feel better.

Sometimes I might say, "Good morning. This is Jean Ziglar's husband." One day when my son was little, I picked up the telephone and said, "Good afternoon. This is Tom Ziglar's dad."

A little boy at the other end said, "Tom there?"

"Sure."

"Can I speak to him?"

"Of course. Tom!"

As I lay the telephone down, the youngster turned to his mother and said, "Boy, they sure have a weird way of answering that telephone."

For a long while after that, every time my car pulled in the driveway, the telephone would ring. After I gave my usual answer, some youngster on the other end would say, "Is Tom there?" He didn't want to talk to Tom. He wanted to hear me answer the telephone.

When your children are between the ages of ten and fifteen, they need you the most but want you the least. At the time when they're subjected to the most peer pressure and need close communication with their parents, they really want it the least. When our son was that age, we created an environment in our home that was loving and friendly. My son's little buddies would come to our house. We would know who they were, and we would know where our son was. No other couple in existence could do as much for Tom Ziglar as Jean and Zig Ziglar, because there's no other couple in existence who loves him the way we do. And we felt the responsibility of making certain that his input was what it should be so that his output later in life would also be at the maximum.

When the telephone rings, you could pick it up and say, "Good morning. It's a great day to start building for a magnificent retirement." Or, "Good morning. It's a great day to start receiving as much money as you deserve." I would develop some teasers, and I'd go to work on building them right there.

I believe that motivational recordings are an absolute must in building your business. According to the University of California, when you drive twelve thousand miles a year alone, in three years' time you can acquire the equivalent of two years of college education. In your car, you can become a master at communication, at closing sales, at motivation, at all of those things.

You need to feed your mind on a deliberate basis. I spent a few minutes once with Mr. Wallace Johnson, one of the co-founders of Holiday Inn. He said, "Zig, there is never a day that goes by when I don't listen to motivational recordings." Mr. H. L. Hunt, worth over a billion dollars at his death, listened to motivational recordings every single day until after he was eighty years old. On at least one of the trips to the moon, the astronauts were listening to motivational recordings. I can tell you with absolute certainty that some of the recordings they were listening to were fantastic. You need to feed your mind. Every day, feed it.

If you're going to reach your goals, you've got to keep your eye on the goal. I'm sure you remember the story of the apostle Peter when Christ walked on the water. There'd been a storm at night, and they looked out and they saw what they thought was a ghost. And then Peter recognized him as Our Lord and he said, "Lord, I would walk on water." And Christ simply said, "Come." And old Peter, I can just visualize him. He is my kind of a guy. You know, nothing was ever mediocre for old Peter. Man, he would say that something was the best in the world or the worst in the world. There was no middle ground. I can just see old Peter when he stepped out of the boat and started towards Christ, walking in big strides, confident. But then the Scriptures say, "But when he saw the wind boisterous, he was afraid, and beginning to sink" (Matthew 14:30). But did you ever wonder why he saw the wind boisterous? Because he took his eyes off the goal. Off the goal which was Jesus Christ.

It makes no difference whether it's a heavenly goal or an earthly goal: when you take your eye off the goal, you see all the woes of society today. But when you're zeroed in on the goal, it's amazing the number of people who will step aside. A man or woman who knows where they're going is going to get a lot of help in getting there, because they see what they want and ignore what they don't want.

It's like the story of the young sailor at sea for the first time. A squall was coming up. As he looked down at the rough waters, he saw the roll of the ship and started to lose his balance and fall. When he did, an older sailor said, "Look up, son." When he did, he regained his balance.

When the outlook isn't good, try the up look. It's always good. If you keep your eyes on the sun, you will never see any shadows. Remember what newspaperman George Matthew Adams said: "He climbs highest who helps another up." Want to reach your goals? Believe in *you*, because you're somebody special. Want to reach your goals? Believe in your fellow human beings, because they too were created in God's own image.

Believe, too, in our great America. Talk to people from other lands, and then make your decision about America. Whether it's the Dutch or British businessman, the Arab oil sheikh, or the Swiss banker, if he's got money to invest, he brings it to America, because it's the greatest land on the face of this earth.

And—which is infinitely more important than anything else—believe in Almighty God, because if you do, you will not only have a good day but a good forever.

SEVEN

Don't Kick the Cat

Once Mr. B, a company owner, called a meeting of all of his people and said, "I noticed that some of you come in to work late. Some of you are spending too much time on a coffee break or on a lunch break. Maybe that's not your fault. Maybe that's my fault. Maybe I've not set for you the kind of an example that I should have been setting, so in the future, I'm going to be the kind of leader you can follow. I'm going to get here early and stay late. I'm going to take short coffee breaks. I'm going to take short lunch breaks. I'm going to provide the kind of leadership that will enable us to build a marvelous company."

It was quite a little speech, and his intentions were good. But about four days later, he was out at the local country club for lunch, and he became engrossed in the business conversation. He forgot about the time and all of a sudden looked at his watch. He said, "Oh, my goodness. I'm due back at the office in ten minutes."

Mr. B made a mad dash to his automobile, hopped in, and burned rubber. He was going ninety miles an hour down the freeway when the long arm of the law entered the picture and gave him a ticket. Mr. B was absolutely furious. He said, "This is ridiculous. Here I am, a peaceful taxpayer, a law-abiding citizen, minding my own business, and what does this guy do? He comes along and gives me a ticket. He ought to be out looking for the robbers, the murderers, the arsonists, the people who are breaking the law. He ought to leave us peaceful taxpayers alone." Oh, he was really upset.

By the time Mr. B got back to the office, about an hour and a half late, he did what management has done since the beginning of time when they get their hand caught in the cookie jar, they say, "Look yonder."

In a very loud voice Mr. B called for the sales manager. He said, "Come on in here. I want to talk to you about the Armstrong account right now. You've been fooling with that thing for six weeks, and I just want you to tell me in one simple word that yes, you made the deal, or no, you did not make the deal."

The sales manager ducked his head, walked in the office, and very meekly and quietly closed the door behind him. He said, "Mr. B, I can tell you this: I thought I had that sale. I thought it was mine. I thought it was all signed, sealed, and delivered. But you know what? At the last minute, something happened, and it came unglued. I don't know what happened, Mr. B, but I lost the sale."

If you think Mr. B was unhappy before, you should have seen him now. He was absolutely furious. He said, "This is ridiculous. For eighteen years, you've been my sales manager. For eighteen years, I've depended on you to bring in new business. Now we have a chance to get the biggest account of all, and what do you do? You blow it. Well, let me tell you, friend, just because you've been here for eighteen years does not mean that you've got a lifetime contract. I'm going to tell you this one time and one time only: you replace that business, or I'm going to replace you." Oh, he was really upset.

But if you think Mr. B was upset, you should have seen that sales manager. He left far from quietly. He walked through the door and slammed it behind him, muttering, "This is ridiculous. For eighteen years, I've been running this company. I'm the only one who knows what's going on around here. Why, if it hadn't been for me, they would have gone down the tube fifteen years ago. Now, just because I lost one miserable deal, he uses a cheap, cotton-picking trick, and he threatens to fire me. This is not fair." Oh, he was really upset.

The sales manager called his secretary in a very loud voice, and said, "Remember those five letters I gave you this morning? Have you gotten them out?

Have you been fiddling around with something else that's not important at all?"

The secretary said, "Why? No, don't you remember? You told me that the Hilliard account took precedence over everything else, and that's what I've been working on. So, no, I have not had a chance to get those letters out."

"Look, don't give any lousy excuses. I told you I wanted those letters out, and I want them out today. I'm just going to tell you this one time. If you can't get them out today, I'm going to get somebody that can. Just because you've been here eight years does not mean that you've got a lifetime contract." Oh, he was really upset.

But if you think the sales manager was upset, you should have seen that secretary. She went out of his office and slammed the door behind her back, muttering, "This is ridiculous. For eight years, I've been at this company. As a matter of fact, I'm the only one who knows what's going on around here. Why, if it hadn't been for me, this company would gone down the tubes seven years ago. Now, just because I can't do two things at once, he uses a cheap, lousy trick: he threatens to fire me. After all the hundreds of hours overtime work I've done and never got a dime in overtime pay. Who does he think he's kidding anyhow?" Oh, she was really upset.

The secretary walked up to the switchboard operator and said, "Look, I've got five letters. Just get them out. Now I know ordinarily that's not your job, but you don't do anything but sit out here and answer the telephone. I want you to get these letters out. And I'm going to tell you this just one time, if you can't get them out, I'm going to get somebody who can." Oh, she was really upset.

But if you think the secretary was upset, you should have seen that switchboard operator. She said, "This is ridiculous. Why, I'm the only one who knows what's going on around here. They don't do anything in the back but gossip, drink coffee, talk on the telephone, and maybe get a little bit of work out. The minute they get behind, they come out here, throw something down on my desk, and say, 'Now you're going to get this out, or we're going to fire you.' Why, if it hadn't been for me, they'd have gone down the tube five years ago. This is ridiculous."

The switchboard operator was really upset, but she got the letters out. When she got home, she was still furious. She walked in the front door and slammed it behind her, muttering under her breath the whole time. The first thing she saw was her twelve-year-old son lying on the floor watching television. The second thing she saw was a big rip right across the seat of his britches. She said, "Son, how many times have I told you, when you come home from school, put your play clothes on? Mother has hard enough time as it is supporting you and sending you through school. Now just for this, you're going to go upstairs right now. There's going to be no supper for you tonight. No television for the next three weeks."

Oh, the operator was really upset. But if you think she was upset, you should have seen that twelve-year-old boy. He hopped up, muttering under his breath, "This is ridiculous. I was doing stuff for my mother. She didn't give me a chance to explain. I had an accident; it could happen to anybody. This is not fair, and she didn't even give me a chance to explain."

About that time, his tomcat walked in front of him, which was a mistake. The boy gave the tomcat a big old boot and said, "You get out of here. You've probably been up to no good yourself."

If you think about it for a moment, that tomcat was the only creature involved that could not have altered that series of events. And if you think about it just that much longer, wouldn't it had been better if Mr. B had just gone directly from the country club to the operator's house and kicked that cat himself?

Now let me ask you a question: whose cat have you been kicking? Let me ask you another question: have you been letting somebody else kick your cat? You see, the truth of the matter is that the billionaire and the bum have got a great deal in common. Every human being, regardless of how big their success or how total their failure, has got a lot in common with everyone else. Each individual who occupies planet earth has faced frustration, disappointment, heartache, and defeat all of their lives. Regardless of their successes or their failures, every living, breathing human being has experienced disappointment, frustration, heartache, and defeat, but the difference between the billionaire and the bum is the way they react to these events.

When the bum meets an obstacle, he says, "Poor little me." The successful person says, "Boy, oh boy. I'm fortunate that I found out early that this wasn't going to work. Now I can go with something that really will." The way we react to the disappointment is the difference between the successful person and the failure. The bum drowns his troubles in drink, only to wake up and discover that all he has drowned is a portion of his life instead of his troubles.

Obviously I'm talking about mental attitude. Have you ever heard anybody tell you that it's important to have a right mental attitude, to eliminate stinking thinking? Really, the purpose of this book is to give you a little checkup from the neck up, because your business is, as a matter of fact, never either good or bad out there. Your business is either good or bad right between your ears. If your thinking is stinking, your business is going to be in the same shape.

There are tens of thousands of schools in America. They'll teach you how to do everything from trim toenails to take out tonsils. They'll teach you how to run heavy equipment or wait on tables. They'll teach you how to shine shoes or do anything that you want to learn how to do. You can learn many things in those schools in America, but there's not a single one anywhere that's going to teach you how to be any better than mediocre unless you've got the right mental attitude.

Mental attitude is the difference between the successful individual and the failure. The truth of the matter is that the difference between the individual who succeeds and the individual who fails is only measured in fractions and inches and seconds. It's not the big things that make the big difference. It's the little things. It's the part of the blanket that hangs over the bed that keeps you warm. If you don't believe that, you've never been in the service and been short-sheeted, I'll tell you that right now.

A long time ago, the philosopher William James said that our mental attitude is the most important factor in our success or our failure, and the attitude we have regarding something is more important than any facts we might have. He taught us two things: first of all, your attitude is important, and second, that you're not stuck with it. Whatever your attitude is now, it's going to change either for the better or for the worse, and this attitude is tremendously important.

Yes, I believe that attitude is important. Some of you might keep up with the races and you might know that the great racehorse Nashwan won over $1 million on the racetracks in less than an hour of actual racing. It took hundreds of hours of training and practice, but only one hour of racing.

Actually, you don't spend that much time conducting business. You spent a lot of time in learning how and where to do it, and whom to conduct business with. You spend a lot of time learning how to deal with the various facets of the business, how to find clients or customers, how to sell to them and meet with them. Yet the few minutes that you spend doing actual business are comparatively few.

Nashwan spent an hour on the racetrack but won over $1 million. Mathematically, this is easy to figure. You can take $1 million, and with it you can buy a hundred $10,000 racehorses, but a million-dollar horse runs exactly a hundred times as fast as a $10,000 one.

Did you believe that? Actually, the million-dollar horse may be only twice as fast, or 10 or even 2 percent faster. How much faster is a million-dollar horse than a $10,000 one? Let me see if I can explain it to you. At the Arlington-Washington Futurity one year, the winning horse received $100,000 more than the horse that came in second place. This race is 1⅛ miles in length, which is 71,280 inches. The winning horse got there exactly one inch in front of the horse that got there in second place. The difference was an inch, a minute fraction, yet it was worth $100,000.

In one year, the winning jockey of the Kentucky Derby received $27,000 as his prize for running his horse across the line. Another jockey crossed the finish line two seconds later, and they wrote him a check for $30.

It's the little things that make the big difference. You can call a girl a kitten, and she'll love you. Call her a cat, and you've got a problem. You can say she is a vision, and you score all kind of points. Call her a sight, and you're in trouble. Imagine a man saying to his wife, "Honey, when I look into your eyes, the wheels of time stand still." That's beautiful. That's poetry. I guarantee you, that will get results. But can you imagine a man looking into his wife's eyes and saying, "Honey, when I look into your eyes, I've got to tell you that you've got a face that could stop a clock." It's not really that much difference, and yet isn't there an enormous difference?

If my watch were four hours wrong, I would have no trouble, because I've got sense enough to tell if it's four hours wrong. But if it's four minutes wrong, I couldn't. Yet I've got a problem, because I fly very often. If I'm catching a plane to Dallas that leaves at 2:20, but if I get there at 2:24—well, let me tell you about the deal I worked out with the airlines. It's a simple deal: it just says that if I'm not there when they're ready to go, they're just to go ahead without me. I recently found out again that they live up to their end of the agreement. I also found out that those dudes are a lot easier to catch before they leave the ground.

The difference between success and failure is not one enormous thing, but a long series of little things that amount to an enormous difference. And of course, attitude is one of those things, because your business is not out there. Your business is right here between your ears.

Once I was speaking to a group of Realtors in Flint, Michigan. At the time, General Motors was on strike. Before I started to speak, I was chatting very pleasantly with a gentleman on my right until I made the most serious mistake of the day: I asked him, "How's business?"

For the next ten minutes this gentleman elaborated on just how bad business was. He said, "Mr. Ziglar, General Motors is on strike. When General Motors is on strike, nobody buys anything from anybody. As a matter of fact, they don't buy any shoes, don't buy any clothes, don't buy any food even. Why, if I don't make a sale soon, I'm going to have to go out of business. It's bad, bad, bad." He was the kind of a guy who could brighten up a whole room by leaving it. Or as they say, "He could frequently be overheard saying nothing."

Finally, somebody came up to him to ask him a question. When they did, I turned to the cute little girl to my left. She was about sixty years old and about four feet, ten inches tall, and couldn't have weighed more than ninety pounds. I said to her, "Well, how's everything?"

"Well, you know, Mr. Ziglar, General Motors is on strike." And I thought, "Oh, brother. I've done it again."

But she finished her sentence with the most beautiful smile and the most marvelous statement as she said, "Still, everything is absolutely fantastic. For the first time in months, people have nothing to do but go shopping for the home of their dreams. They are not working, so they can spend all day long looking even at just one house or two houses. Some of them go up in the attic, and they'll start to check the insulation. They'll check every square inch. They'll check the closets. They'll even check the foundations." She went on, "They know the strike is going to end. They have faith in the economy of America, and they know that right now they can buy a house cheaper than they're ever going to be able to buy one again." Then she got confidential and said, "Mr. Ziglar, do you know anybody down in Washington?"

"Why yes, ma'am," I said. "As a matter of fact, I've got a nephew in school down there right now."

"No, no. I mean, do you know anybody down there with some political muscle?"

"Why, no, I really don't. But I'm curious: why do you ask?"

"Well, I was just thinking that if you knew somebody down there who could keep this strike going just six more weeks, I would be able to retire, because my business has been fantastic ever since it has been on."

Let me emphasize the point. A man was going broke because the strike was on. A lady was getting rich because the strike was on. You see, it wasn't the situation; it was the way they reacted to the situation.

How do you react to the negative? Say you go into a restaurant for a cup of coffee, and you sit there and sit there, and finally you say, "Miss, could I have a cup of coffee?"

She says, "Can't you see that I'm busy? I'll get you in a minute."

What do you do? Do you say, "You don't have to bite my head over about it, do you?" Do you let them pull you down to their level? Or can you understand that somebody has been there kicking her cat before you ever got there?

Have you ever gotten caught in a traffic jam? Traffic three blocks in front, traffic three blocks behind you, and some idiot right behind you sits on the horn. Do you turn around and say, "Can't you see they've got traffic in front of us?" Again, do you let them pull you down to their level?

Sometimes you might try to talk to somebody about your product, and he gets uptight about it. He replies, "Don't talk to me about anything like that. Why, that's nothing but a bunch of bull." Can you understand that it may be because somebody had kicked his cat before you ever got there?

Or maybe you come home from work having had a super day, when everything went 100 percent right. You walk in the front door whistling, and you ask your wife, "Hi, honey. How are you doing?" And she says, "What do you mean, how I'm doing? You should have been here forty-five minutes ago. If you'd been dealing with this mess all day long, you wouldn't be feeling so good either." Can you understand, fellows, that this has got nothing to do with you? Somebody's been kicking her cat all day long.

Do you realize we live in a negative, cat-kicking world? And if we're not careful, we will become part of what we are around.

When an individual gets turned on, they don't let anybody else kick their cat. They understand completely that man was designed for accomplishment. That he's engineered for success. That he's endowed with the seeds of greatness. Because they believe this and they develop the right mental attitude, they are able to accomplish much more.

As I pointed out once, "God said to build a better world. How? The world is such a cold, dark place, and I'm so small and useless. There's nothing I can do, but God in all his wisdom said, 'Just build a better you.'"

That's in reality what we are talking about, not doing something that lies dimly in the distant future, over the horizon, but doing something about *you* right now, where you are, with what you've got. That's what really builds a better you. Which means we also build a better America.

EIGHT

Four Steps to a Positive Attitude

've had the privilege of speaking to many major league baseball teams, as well as to schools, churches, corporations, and financial institutions—just about every kind of organization known to man. Without exception, corporate executives, coaches, teachers, and parents all say that having the right mental attitude is tremendously important for success.

I want to share with you a very specific formula that will teach you exactly how to control your attitude. Sometimes when things are going well, you think, "Boy, if I could always feel this way, I could turn this world upside down." I want to tell you exactly how to do that.

I'm going to give you a formula in four steps. It's not going to take any time, require any effort, or cost any money. Many people invest in clothing; they think that's important. Or haircuts. Or trips to the beauty shop. The cost of this formula is less than zero, but will do two things: first of all, you'll immediately make more money. Second, you will immediately have more fun.

Before I share the formula with you, I've got to tell you a little bit about the way the mind works. It's actually a very simple process. The mind is pretty much like a garden. You know that if you want to raise beans, you don't plant potatoes. If you want to raise beans, you've got to plant beans, because whatever you plant is going to come up. That's a fact.

The mind is the same way. Whatever you plant is going to come up. You cannot plant negatives and reap positives. You've got to plant positives if you want to reap positives.

Previously I mentioned the fact that we were going to bury the garbage that has been accumulating in your mind over a period of years. Unfortunately, we're going to cover it only with a thin layer. The first time you encounter a little negative thinking from somebody else, some of that garbage breaks up through the thin veneer, and now you've got stinking thinking again.

As I've also said, we're going to put a few more layers over that old garbage until we finally cover all of it. We're going to bury it forever, but the minute you get all the old garbage completely buried, some-body comes along and dumps two fresh loads into a good clean mind.

I want to teach you how to bury the fresh garbage and keep the old garbage completely submerged. The way the mind works, whatever you put in is going to come out. But understand that you can't make an overdraft on the bank of mental attitude all of your life and expect to bring the account up to date with one deposit. That's where we make such a serious mistake. A person may go negative after one injection. We need to give them another injection, and then another, and another, so one of these days, they'll get the message. You can send a message twenty-five thousand miles around the world in less than a tenth of a second, but sometimes it takes years for it to go that last quarter of an inch. So you need to make more than just one deposit.

What would you do or what would you think if I were to come into your home with a pail of garbage and dump it on your living room floor? You'd either get your gun and say, "Now, Ziglar, you better clean that up," you'd whip me physically, or you'd call the law and have me arrested. The truth of the matter is, though, I could take some good carpet cleaner and clean it up without any difficulty at all.

When people dump garbage in your mind, that's far more serious. What about these people that dump negativism into our mind? How upset do we get then?

What you put into the mind can either help you or hurt you. If it's positive, it builds. If it's negative, it destroys.

So let's look at a formula. As I've said, it's a very simple formula. It doesn't take any time, it's not going to involve any effort, is not going to cost any money, and will require no more energy than is required to run up and down a flight of stairs.

There is a catch, however. The part that is a little negative is that if you follow the formula I'm now going to give you, you're going to be slightly embarrassed for as long as two minutes a day in front of your mate.

Tomorrow morning when the alarm sounds off, you've got to reverse the way you get out of bed. Now you're not going to get out of bed backwards. But when that alarm clock sounds off, many people rub their eyes a little bit, slap their face a time or two, and say, "Is it 7:00 already? It seems like I just went to bed. I've got that 9:00 appointment, but that person isn't going to buy anything. No way."

Many people start every day as if it's going to be another yesterday, and they weren't overly excited about yesterday. But tomorrow morning, when that alarm clock sounds off, reach over, shut it off, sit straight up on the side of bed, clap your hands, and say, "Oh, boy, it's a magnificent day to get up and go to work!"

Now I want you to get the picture. There you are, on the side of the bed. Your hair is hanging down over your eyes. You're clapping your hands, you're acting like an eight-year-old child and saying, "Oh, boy, it's a good day to get out and go to work!" If you live to be 168, you will never tell a bigger whopper than that. But you are up, and that is where you wanted to be when you set the alarm.

When you set the alarm, you decided, "I'm going to get up tomorrow morning at 7:00." When the alarm goes off, you don't decide again. You're going to get up. You've decided that. All you're going to decide now is *how* you're going to get up. You can get up as you've been doing it, or you can get up as if it's another magnificent day.

As the Bible says, "This is the day which the Lord hath made; we will rejoice and be glad in it" (Psalm 118:24). Solomon says, "He that is of a merry heart hath a continual feast" (Proverbs 15:15). So it's scripturally sound when we say, "Get up whooping and shouting and hollering."

Another thing that this practice does: it eliminates and overcomes procrastination. It does something else too. It starts putting you in control of the situation instead of letting the situation control you.

The truth of the matter is, everybody has got a good attitude after they've had a success. Everybody has got a good attitude when things are going well. That's no big deal. What about when things are not going well?

When things are not going well, that's when the attitude is in trouble. I'm talking now about building an attitude foundation so solid that when things are good, you've got a good attitude, and when things are bad, you've still got a good attitude, which means that soon things will be good.

When you're sitting on the side of your bed, it's doubly beneficial if there's a big mirror in front of you, so you can see just how ridiculous you look. I don't believe there's a normal human being alive who can look at that sight and not get hysterical. What you'll be laughing at is you, and as long as you can laugh at *you*, it doesn't upset you if somebody else laughs at you.

If you happen to be married, it's doubly beneficial if your wife or your husband does this exercise with you. Now you've got a double comedy in living color.

When you sow an action, you reap a habit. When you sow a habit, you reap character. And when you sow character, you reap a destiny. But I'm digging a great deal deeper even than that. You see, every good habit known to man—whether it's tithing, saving money, or being kind to the mate that you profess to love and cherish—is difficult to grab. You've got to grab it and hold on to it for dear life.

But every bad or destructive habit—regardless of what it is, whether it's obesity, profanity, promiscuity, drugs, drinking, or smoking—was acquired slowly and gradually. You were unaware of the fact that you were gaining an ounce a day until at the end of the year, you realized that you had gained twenty-three pounds. You acquired the habit so slowly that before you know you've got the habit, the habit has got you.

Let me give you a couple of examples. France has the highest rate of alcoholism in the world. They have the highest rate of wine consumption in the world. Think that's a coincidence? Chile has the second highest rate of alcoholism in the world. They've got the second highest rate of wine consumption in the world. Think that's a coincidence?

In the years since they've been doing the hard sell on cheap wines on television, teenage alcoholism has skyrocketed so spectacularly that they cannot even keep up with the inquiries. I've done a lot of work in the drug war. I've never met a kid mainlining heroin who told me in all sincerity that when he lit the first joint, it was his goal to become an addict. I have never talked to an alcoholic who told me that when they had that first beer as a teenager, it was their objective to become an alcoholic. I've never talked to a person who was 150 pounds overweight who told me that as a youngster it was their objective to become obese. I've never talked to an individual with a destructive habit of this nature who said, "This is what I started out to be."

The changes of habit are too weak to be felt until they're too strong to be broken. The habit that you were not going to get eventually gets you. That's why one person out of sixteen who takes an occasional drink will become an alcoholic. Regardless of what they are, your bad habits are acquired slowly, but you've got to reach up and grab your good habits.

This is absurd. It's ridiculous. There you are, grown, intelligent, educated, successful, mature, and I'm suggesting to you that you get up and clap your hands like an eight-year-old child. But I can guarantee that on the first day, you're going to have a benefit. I'll guarantee you will feel silly, but you will catch yourself laughing about it. Anything that will make you laugh can't be all bad. Besides, you'll be laughing at *you*. That's the surest sign of a healthy self-image.

Next, I suggest that you go in the bathroom, take your shower, and sing. Sing loudly. Don't worry about whether or not you can carry a tune. Mitch Miller wrote me a personal letter once asking me not even to bother to sing along with him. William James, the father of American psychology, said, "We do not sing because we're happy. We are happy because we sing." Physical action speeds mental acceptance.

Step number one is getting up and singing in the shower. Step number two: establish some symbols. In America we've got symbols all over, thousands and thousands of them, on every street corner. Now some people call them red lights. Some people call them stoplights. Some people call them traffic lights. But you have agreed that you're going to call them *go lights*. The average human being spends twenty-seven hours every year waiting on the right color in front of the go lights. How do most people spend those hours? You're not going to believe this, but some of them will actually rev up the motor, because it'll make the light change faster. If you think it's silly to get up in the morning and clap your hands, what about revving up the motor to change the color of the light?

I've got a good friend in Winnipeg, Canada, who is the most positive man that I've ever met in my life. He is so positive that he's never had a cold. Occasionally does have a warm. He's so positive that he never even talks about the weekend because that's negative. He calls it the "strong end."

You might be saying now, "Ziglar, come on. Get up. Clap your hands. Talk about go lights. Or colds and warms and strong ends and weekends. Is all of that stuff necessary?" No, it's not necessary. You can be mediocre without it.

But I'm suggesting that the way to succeed is to be a cut above the average individual that you deal with every day. You don't have to be that much above, but a little here and a little there, and this gives you that extra edge.

What do you do when you pull up in front of the go light? You look at it and say, "That's put there for me so that I can go faster and more smoothly, easily, and safely to my destination."

Step number three: set your gyroscope. As I've said, it's amazing to me the number of people who answer the telephone as if it's an interruption. They pick it up and say, "Yes?" Or, "Hello." Or, "This is John; can I help you?"

Why don't you pick that telephone up as if it's the most exciting instrument you have? Because it is. It establishes contact with either a future, potential, or current customer. Everybody fits into one of those three categories. When you pick up that telephone, why not say something like, "Oh, good morning to you"? Why don't you to pick up that telephone as if you're excited about life and can't wait to talk to whoever did you the honor of calling? This is building your attitude.

So you answer the telephone enthusiastically, and when you are talking, you write down, "I can, I can, I can." Write down your goal on a sheet of paper. Write it on the bathroom mirror. Burn it indelibly into your subconscious mind.

The fourth step to control that attitude of yours is to feed your mind. Everything that you learn, you learn consciously. But if you're going to do something well, you've got to learn to do it subconsciously. Somebody asks, "How are you doing?" If you've got to think about how you're doing, you're not doing so well. When somebody says, "How are you doing?" you can, should, and will learn how to instinctively, automatically say, "Doing super good, but I'll get better." You can move it from the conscious mind into the subconscious mind.

When you learn anything, initially you have to learn it consciously. If you learned how to drive an automobile with a stick shift, do you remember how you first had to learn consciously how to mash the clutch in? Then you said, "Now, shift the gear." Then you said, "Now, foot on the accelerator." Then you said, "Now, ease out on the car." You were a menace to society.

A few weeks later, as you would mash in the clutch, shift the gear, and put your food on the accelerator, you could roll down the window, light a cigarette, throw out the match, and talk about your neighbors all at the same time. You remembered how to do it because you had moved it from the conscious into the subconscious mind.

I get excited when I think about the power of the mind and what we can do with it. Let me suggest a book, although it's fairly heavy. It was written by a Dutch psychiatrist named Joost A. Meerloo, and it's entitled *The Rape of the Mind*. In this book, he tells how during the Korean War, the North Koreans would take our young GI prisoners of war and subject them to brainwashing techniques. Two of their communistic indoctrinators would go to work on a young GI, twenty or twenty-one years old. They'd start pumping that garbage in for ten to twelve hours. Then the North Koreans would get two fresh indoctrinators, who would go on for ten or twelve hours more, then two more fresh ones, and so on. Finally, after several days of this—often after complete physical, mental, and emotional exhaustion—the young GI would throw in the towel and say, "All right." Although he had bitterly resisted, those lies were forced into his mind thousands upon thousands of times, so he ended up believing something that he had initially rejected.

These prisoners started out fighting, but the power of the spoken word, repeated into their minds over and over, overcame their resistance. Now there was one exception: those young GIs who had strong religious convictions. They were able to withstand the brainwashing.

If you read Isaiah 40:31, you'll know why. That verse says, "But they that wait upon the LORD shall renew their strength; they shall mount up with wings as eagles; they shall run, and not be weary; and they shall walk, and not faint." In the original Hebrew, the word for *renew* means *to change* or *exchange*. When you serve God, you change or exchange your strength for his. The young GIs could not resist, but when God enters the picture, you've got the eternal arithmetic that says that you plus God equals enough.

That's a negative example. I've already given you a positive example: the Suzuki method for learning the violin.

I'm suggesting to you that if every day of your life you use audio recordings or the printed word to put good things into your mind, over a period of time you will feed that mind so totally that you will end up being positive about every phase of your life. I believe that if we bathe our minds in love, if we wash them every day in affection, if we surround them with care, if we associate with right-thinking people, if we surround ourselves with the right mental attitude for ourselves, for our families, for our business, for our country, I believe we can go anywhere we want to go. I believe we can do what we want to do. I believe that we can make America's tomorrow so much greater than its yesterdays that the world will be astonished, not at what we've done in the past, but at what we're doing now and are going to do in the future. I believe America's best days are ahead.

If we want to gain control of that mind of ours, we need to use this little four-step formula. We only do the first part for twenty-one days: for twenty-one days, we get up, clap our hands, and whoop and shout and holler. But from now on, we need to be permanently conscious of the go lights. From now on, we need to be conscious of every time we're on the telephone, saying, "I can, I can, I can." From now on, we need to read inspirational books and listen to recordings.

It's amazing, the number of people who say, "I like to listen to those audios when I'm down." That's good, and they'll help you get you up, but did you know that they're even more beneficial when you're already higher than a kite? You know why? A lot of times when you're down and you hear somebody come out with some marvelous ideas, you'll say, "That doesn't apply to me." You summarily reject a lot of things as not being applicable. But when you're high, your imagination is going, and you're enthusiastic, turned on, and motivated, you dare to dream.

That's why in America today, we have dreamers who are building foundations, so every day, whether you're high or low, you need to feed the mind with good, pure, powerful, and positive things.

Let me give a little warning here. I'm talking about a departure for you. I'm talking about a way of life, adopting a philosophy and doing some things that might require mental adjustment. If you carry out this process for twenty-one days, it will make a dramatic change in your life. I've got thousands of letters in my files that say, "I followed that procedure. The results are spectacular."

I'm not giving you a theory. I'm not talking about something that I think might work *maybe, if.* I'm talking about something that has worked many times over a period of years for people of all ages, races, creeds, and colors. I'm talking about a procedure that will help you to build a huge success.

Another warning: when you start doing these things, a certain segment of this population around you is going to look at you and say, "Boy, that guy is different." Or, "Boy, that girl is different."

Of course they'll be right. You've made a choice. You have decided you'd rather be different than nothing. You're going to be one of the five people in a hundred who get what they want instead of having to want what they've got.

Yes, you're going to be different all right. Some people are even going to criticize you. But friends, let me tell you something: since the beginning of time, nobody has ever erected a statue to a critic, so I wouldn't be too concerned about the criticism.

And isn't it amazing how as you grow, build, develop, acquire, and accumulate, the criticism turns to envy? "I wish I'd gotten started then, before it was too late." Others will say, "It's too early to see how it's going to do. The people in this town won't buy this idea. Wait until you get something started, and then come back and see me." Then you come back six months or a year later, and they say, "Yeah, just my luck. I always wait until it's too late. Everybody's in." Have you ever noticed that?

Many people are like the little boy who had a piece of candy, and he was just eating away. Two other boys were with him. One of them said, "I want some of that candy."

"I'm not going to going to give you anything. If you haven't been so greedy and asked for it, I would have given you some, but since you did, I'm not going to do it." He kept eating his candy.

As he took the last bite, the other little boy said, "I didn't ask you for any."

"Yeah, I know you didn't. I didn't think you wanted it. That's why I didn't give you any."

That little boy had an answer for everything. Many people who don't make it in life have got their own reasons. But I'm not talking about a reason for not doing it. I'm talking about ways to do it.

Some people are going laugh at you. The little world laughed, but the big world gathered on the banks of the Hudson when Robert Fulton went steaming by. The little world laughed, but the big world watched when the Wright brothers made the historic flight that changed the course of mankind. The little world might laugh, and did laugh, but the big world was tuned in when Alexander Graham Bell made the historic phone call that opened the lines of communication all over. The little world might laugh when you start out on your journey, but I'll guarantee the big world is going to be right at the finish line, cheering you across.

When you come across, I'll be able to look you dead center and say, "What you have become by reaching your destination is infinitely more important than what you have gotten by reaching your destination."

Follow this formula, and then I truly will see you at the top.

NINE

The Message of the Pump

et me start with a story about two guys named Rick and Tom. Rick went out one day and bought a horse for $1,000. As he was showing it to Tom, Tom said, "Man," said, "that is some horse. I'll give you $1,500 for it."

Rick liked to turn a buck, so said, "OK, Tom, you got yourself a deal."

No sooner had Rick made the sale than it dawned on him that Tom was a pretty shrewd judge of horse-flesh, so he thought, "That guy knows something I don't know. I've got to get that horse back." So Rick went to Tom and said, "I'd give you $2,000 for that horse back."

Tom liked to turn a buck too, so he said, "OK. You got yourself a deal."

No sooner had Tom sold that horse back to Rick for $2,000 than it occurred to him that Rick must know something he didn't know about that horse. So Tom said, "Rick, I'll tell you what I'll do. I've been thinking about that horse. I want it back. I'll give you $3,000 for him."

Rick didn't think he could go broke turning a profit, so he let the horse go for $3,000, but when that happened, he got nervous again. "You know, Tom is nobody's dummy. He wouldn't be giving him $3,000 for a horse that did not have value."

Rick went to Tom and said, "Tom, I'll give you $4,000 for that horse back."

No sooner had he done that than it created another problem. Rick and Tom went back and forth until that horse sold for over $12,000. Rick made the last purchase.

Tom thought, "This got to stop. I'm going to go to that guy, and I'm going to make him one last offer. We're going close this thing out." So Tom went to Rick and said, "I'll give you $15,000 for the horse. Now this is the last time. No more horse trading."

Rick said, "Tom, I'd like to sell him to you, but it's too late."

"What do you mean it's too late?"

"A guy stopped by just an hour ago and gave me $16,000 for the horse."

"Don't tell me you sold it!"

"Why, certainly. It was at a profit."

"You idiot! We were both making a good living on that horse, and you cut a stranger in on the deal."

Anyway, I'm convinced beyond any reasonable doubt that there ain't no free lunch. It's true that Washington is putting a lot of them out on consignment, but sooner or later somebody is going to have to pay for those lunches. Tragically, the people who are receiving them are the ones who will pay the highest price, because there truly ain't no free lunch.

I want to talk about work now. I think the greatest privilege we have in America today is the privilege of work. As a child of the Depression, I saw an older brother leave home every day seeking work, any kind of work, doing anything, only requiring that he be honest. I've seen husbands and fathers desperately seeking employment. I've seen the sheer ecstasy, the thrill beyond belief, of the person who got a job and came home to their family and said, "Today I got a job." I've seen tears of joy wept over and over when somebody has gotten a job.

In my judgment, this privilege of working as long as you wish, as hard as you wish, and as enthusiastically as you wish is one of the great privileges that we have. I'm convinced that the Bible is 100 percent right when it says, "Work so that you might have everything." Now, *everything* covers a lot of territory. Work is a wonderful, marvelous privilege.

I love the story of the farmer who was an awfully hard worker. He had some boys that he worked just as hard as he did. One day a neighbor said to him, "John, you don't have to work these boys that hard to raise a crop." The farmer looked at him and said, "You apparently don't understand. I'm not raising a crop, I'm raising boys." The truth of the matter is, we've got to be before we can have.

I have a chrome-plated pump. I've noticed something rather unusual: when I get aboard an aircraft carrying this pump, almost without exception I am the only passenger who has one. So I've got to assume that there is a shortage of chrome-plated pumps.

One day I stepped aboard an aircraft with this pump, and a stewardess said to me, "What is that?"

I flippantly said, "It's a pump."

"What do you do with it?"

"I pump."

There is a plaque on it that says, "To Zig, America's Number One Flea Trainer." The stewardess read it aloud and asked, "Do you train fleas?"

"I certainly do."

"How do you train fleas?"

"I'll tell you what: when we're airborne, come over to my seat, and I'll explain to you how we train fleas."

Later she enthusiastically came to me and asked, "How do you train fleas?"

I explained to her that a flea trainer was an individual who jumps out of the jar, who is driven from within, who understands that you can get everything in life that you want if you will just help enough other people get what they want. I explained her that a flea trainer does not tell others where to get off but shows them how to get on. I explained to her that a flea trainer does not try to see through people; a flea trainer tries to see people through. I explained to her that a flea trainer is not influenced by surrounding negative influences, but is motivated and driven from within. A flea trainer jumps out of the jar and removes those ceilings.

When I finished explaining what a flea trainer was, the stewardess leaned over and kissed me on the forehead. As she stood up, with a trace of a tear in her eyes, she said, "You know, for all of my life I've wanted to be a stewardess. I've only been one for a short period of time. It's been a very miserable experience. Oh, it's not that I don't love my work, because I truly do. But my family has brought such unbelievable pressure to bear on me that I was about to quit today.

"As a matter of fact, they've made life so miserable every day of my life that today I have packed my bags. They are aboard this aircraft. This was to have been my last flight."

Then she straightened up perceptibly and said, "But I'm not going to quit. I love the work. I love being a stewardess. And for me, it is right. For me, it is good. I'm going to stay with this." As a matter of fact, she said, "I'm going to be a flea trainer."

Let me return to the pump, because I believe that this pump is the story of your life. I believe this pump is the story of America. I believe fervently that if you don't learn anything else from this book but the message of this pump, it will help you go where you want to go, do what you want to do, and be as you want to be.

A number of years ago, a couple of good friends of mine were down in south Alabama. It was a hot August day, and they were riding around. It was terribly hot and they got thirsty. This was in the days before air-conditioned automobiles. They saw an old, abandoned farmhouse. Bernard Haygood was driving. He pulled behind this old abandoned farmhouse and saw an old pump. He hopped out with his brother-in-law, Jimmy Glen, and he ran over, grabbed the pump, and started to pump.

Bernard had been pumping a couple of minutes when he said, "Jimmy, you're going to have to get that old bucket over there and get some water out of the creek. We're going to have to prime the pump." This means that you've got to put some water in at the top before you can get some water out.

Isn't this the story of life? Don't you know a lot of people who stand in front of the stove and say, "Stove, if you give me some heat, then I'll put some wood in you"? Don't you know a lot of secretaries who say, "Boss, give me a raise, and then I'll start coming to work on time"? How many times do we hear people say, "First of all, you reward me, and then I'll perform"?

It doesn't work that way. The farmer will tell you that before he can raise the crop, he's got to plant the seeds. Before he can reap the harvest, he's got to cultivate and irrigate the crop, or let the Lord irrigate it.

Bernard wanted that drink of water. He was thirsty. South Alabama does get awfully hot. He was pumping back and forth and up and down, and he was really working up a sweat.

The question invariably arises of just how much pumping you're willing to do in order to get a drink of water. Finally, Bernard said, "You know, Jimmy, I just don't believe there's any water down there."

"Yeah, there is, Bernard," said Jimmy. "You know, in south Alabama, the wells are deep. We're glad they are, because the deep wells are the ones that produce the good, clean, sweet, pure, best-tasting water of all."

Isn't this too the story of life? Isn't it true that the person who is going to be an outstanding producer is one who is dedicated, enthusiastic, and conscientious? Isn't true that we have to do an awful lot of pumping? Isn't it true that the boy or the girl who is the ideal mate is the one who says no to the average Tom, Dick, Jane, or Mary that comes down the pike, saving themselves and saying, "I'm special for a special man or a special woman"? The things in life that really have value are the things for which you have to do a lot of pumping.

Bernard wanted that drink of water. There were no two ways about it. He was thirsty, he was sweating, and he was pumping away, but again the inevitable question is going to arise: just how much pumping are you willing to do for one drink of water? Finally,

Bernard threw his hands up in the air and said, "Jimmy," he said, "There just ain't any water down there."

"Bernard, don't quit," said Jimmy. "If you do, the water goes all the way back down, and then you're going to have to start all over."

Isn't this the story of life too? There's no way we can look at a pump and say, "Yup, two more strokes, and then I've got it." Because it might be ten feet down; it might take an awful lot of pumping. But this we do know: if we pump long enough, hard enough, and enthusiastically enough, eventually it is going to bring forth the reward, which always follows the effort.

We also know something else, don't we? We know that once we get that water flowing, all we've got to do is keep a little easy, steady pressure on it, and we're going to have more water than we know what to do with.

Isn't this too the story of life? Isn't it true that when things are good, they invariably get better? And when they're bad, they invariably get worse? It's got nothing whatever to do with what's going on out there, because your business is never either good or bad *out there*. Your business is either good or bad right between your own two ears. If your thinking is stinking, your business is going to be in exactly the same shape.

I love the story of the pump because it says so much about life. It has nothing to do with your age. It has nothing to do with your education, with whether you're black or white or Catholic or Jewish, with whether you're overweight or underweight. This is your God-given right as a free individual: to work as long as you wish, as enthusiastically as you wish and as hard as you wish to get what you deserve in the game of life.

I believe the pump says a lot of things, and I do a lot of pumping. I want you to understand that in the game of life, you're going to find all kinds of people: your dropouts and your copouts, your washouts and your fallouts. You're going to have your cry-outs, your way-outs, your get-outs, and these people invariably become the miss-outs.

Let me tell you something: whatever anybody else does, you can have a positive influence on them, but don't let them steal your dream. You've come too far. You've seen too much. You know deep down, within every fiber of your being, that you can succeed by working enthusiastically and following a plan.

I get excited when I hear people talking about commitment. I believe fervently that as we move up our stairway to the top, commitment involves desire. I believe you've got to really want success. I believe you've got to want the good things of life. I believe you've got to want them beyond some of the other things in life.

To return to a point I made earlier: I want to correct a statement that I have made for many years. For years, I've gone around this country and I've said,

"You've got to pay the price." I've said it, I guess, ten thousand times. If you ever heard me say it, let me beg you: forgive me for misleading you.

At this point, I'm convinced beyond any reasonable doubt that you do not pay a price for happiness. You do not pay a price for success. You do not pay a price for accomplishment, for good health. All we've got to do is to compare the successful person with the failure, the happy person with the miserable one, the person who doesn't have good health with those who do have good health, to discover that you pay the price for failure, and you enjoy the price of success.

You've got to make a commitment. When I think about desire, when I think about climbing up that stairway to the top, I think about Pete Gray. Pete Gray, for my money, is a baseball immortal. When he was a very young man, he had an overwhelming desire. He said, "One of these days I'm going to play major league ball. One of these days I'm going all the way to the big top. I'm going to play a game in Yankee Stadium."

Finally in 1945, playing for the St. Louis Browns, Pete Gray made it all the way to the major leagues. He never hit a home run. He only lasted one year. He was not even a regular. But I fervently believe that Pete Gray is an immortal who belongs in the Baseball Hall of Fame. Because Pete Gray made it all the way to the big top with just one good arm. Not once did he ever look down and say, "This I do not have." He kept looking up and saying, "This I do have." He did not let what he did not have keep him from using what he did have.

That's what success is. It's not determined by having been dealt a good hand. It's determined by taking the hand that you were dealt and using it to the very best of your ability.

When you do have that overwhelming desire, you're going to develop what I call *intelligent ignorance*. You will not know what you *cannot* do.

Many times, people say, "I will make it if my wife will cooperate. I will make it if my children will cooperate. I will make it if the people around here will just respond. I will *if, if, if*." Take the word *if* and the word *life*, and you will discover that half of *life* is *if*; it's the middle half. People who make *if* commitments have made no commitments whatsoever. You've got to be committed. You've got to determine what you're going to do, because this is what develops intelligent ignorance.

When I think of intelligent ignorance, I think about Henry Ford. He had already revolutionized the automobile industry by instituting $5 a day wages (which were unheard-of then), setting up assembly line production, and putting the working people of America into affordable transportation. He was responsible for billions of dollars in growth in this country.

One day, Henry Ford had an idea. He said, "I'm going to build a V-8 engine." He called his engineers together and said, "Gentlemen, I want you to build a V-8 engine for me."

They looked at him as if the old man had lost his marbles. They said, "Mr. Ford, it's an engineering impossibility. It cannot be done."

Henry Ford said, "Gentlemen, you don't understand. We've got to have it now. Go build it."

The engineers went to work, came back shortly, and said, "It cannot be done."

Henry Ford said, "You don't understand. We've got to have it. Go build it."

They tried again, and for the third time, they came back and said, "Mr. Ford, it cannot be done."

"Gentlemen," he said, "apparently you do not understand. I must have a V-8 engine, and you must build it now without any further delay. I say, go build the V-8 engine."

This time the engineers built the V-8 engine—because one man said that it could and would be done.

Intelligent ignorance is what the bumblebee possesses. Anyone who can read understands that the bumblebee cannot fly. Its body is too heavy. Its wings are too light. Aerodynamically, it's a physical impossibility, but the bumblebee does not read. The bumblebee flies. Intelligent ignorance enables you to take life's lemons and make lemonade out of them.

Charles Goodyear had a lemon. It was a prison sentence. He was sent to jail for a contempt of court charge. He got himself assigned to the kitchen, and while there, he discovered the process for vulcanizing rubber. Yes, when we have those lemons, we can make lemonade.

I love the story of Gene Tunney, one of the greatest heavyweight champions who ever stepped into the squared circle. Gene Tunney never would have been the heavyweight champion of the world if he had not broken both of his hands. As a very young man, he was a light heavyweight. During World War I, he was fighting with the American Expeditionary Forces in France and broke both of his hands. His trainer said to him, "Tunney, you'll never be the heavyweight champion. Your hands are too brittle." His doctor said to him, "These hands will not take the heavy pounding that a puncher demands."

Tunney started his boxing career as a puncher. He could knock a man out with either his left or his right. When those hands were broken, his doctor and trainer did not feel he could ever be the heavyweight champion, but Gene Tunney said, "Gentlemen, I'm going to be the heavyweight champion of the world. I'm going to learn how to box, and I'll win the championship."

History will tell you that when Tunney stepped into the squared circle with Jack Dempsey, he took the heavyweight championship on points. He had become one of the most skillful boxers to ever step into the ring. Experts will tell you today that had Gene Tunney not broken his hands—had he tried to slug it out with Jack Dempsey—he never would have been the heavyweight champion of the world. He took his lemon, which was two broken hands, and made it his lemonade: the heavyweight championship of the world.

On occasions, you're going to say, "Well, Lord, now you've given me this lemon, and all I've got to do is get busy and make some lemonade." I'm persuaded that not only can you make lemonade, but you can make it pink, if that happens to be your favorite color.

One reasons I love the Bible is that it has so many positive thinking stories in it. I'm always amused by the people who say, "Well, I'd read the Bible, but I just don't understand it." I'm convinced it's not the part they don't understand that bothers them, because God does speak very clearly. For example, he did not call them the Ten Suggestions.

As I said, I love the Bible, because it's full of positive thinking and people with intelligent ignorance. I think David had a great deal of intelligent ignorance. You remember the story: here's old nine-foot Goliath, weighing four hundred pounds. He is standing there, and he's shouting and cursing; he's blaspheming the Lord and says, "Come on out, you dogs, and fight."

Here comes little David, seventeen years old. He runs out there, and his brothers are standing around, as is the army. David said, "Whoa, whoa, whoa. What's that fellow saying?"

"He's challenging us to fight."

"Aren't you going to take him up on it?"

"Why? Are you crazy? People get hurt fighting guys like that."

David said, "I'll take him on."

They said, "You're crazy."

You see, they looked at Goliath and figured he was too big to hit. David looked at him and figured he was too big to miss.

David said, "Where is the king?"

They said, "King no feel so good."

David said, "I'm going to take that giant on for sure."

Again, his companions thought he was crazy. They looked at Goliath and compared Goliath to them, and that made Goliath awfully big. David looked at Goliath and compared him to God, and that made Goliath awfully small.

I've never heard this story put more completely in perspective than by my son when he was only eight years old. We were on a trip down to San Antonio, and I was telling him the story of David and Goliath. I said to him, "Son, that David was really a brave boy, wasn't he?"

With a look of some disgust, he said, "Well, yeah, Dad, David was brave, but Goliath was really the brave one."

"Well, boy," I asked, "how do you explain that? What do you mean?"

My son got a little provoked. He looked at me and said, "Well, Daddy, you've got to understand. Goliath was out there by himself. But you said David had God with him."

When you put things in perspective, that's exactly what I'm talking about. And you know some of my Christian brothers sometimes don't put things in perspective. They don't have any trouble with Genesis 1:1: "In the beginning God created the heavens and the earth." That's easy. They believe that, no problem. They don't have any difficulty believing that God split the Red Sea so the nearly three million Israelites could go across. They have no difficulty believing that the Lord walked on water, but then they think, "Lord, I've got this car payment next Wednesday. And that's just too tough for you to handle."

I'm going to tell you a story that I believe is going to say everything that I've been attempting to say throughout this book. Once I was speaking in Kansas City. I finished on Saturday afternoon, and it was too late to get back to my home in Columbia, South Carolina, that evening.

I was staying in the Muehlebach Hotel. I went upstairs to shower and change clothes. I came down, and as I stepped off the elevator, I heard the booming voice of a man whom I've come to love as a brother. You could have heard this voice for three blocks. He said, "Zig, where are you going?"

"Bernie," I said, "I'm going to dinner."

"I'll make you a deal. If you'll come and go to dinner with me, I'll buy."

I have a standard policy: when somebody offers to buy my dinner, I let them. So I said, "OK, Bernie, let's go."

We went to dinner and sat down, and we started to chat. We established a rapport that was almost instant because we had so many similarities all the way through our lives.

"Bernie," I said, "you've certainly come a long way to attend the sales rally."

"Yes, indeed. Am I ever glad that I did."

"You had to spend some bucks to get here."

"That's true," he said, "but really, Zig, I don't have to worry about money, thanks to my son, David."

"Bernie, that sounds like a story."

"It is."

"Would you share it?"

"I'd be delighted to. You know, Zig, when our son was born, our joy knew no bounds. We already had our two daughters. Now that we had our son, the family was complete.

"But it wasn't very long before we realized that something was wrong. His head hung too limply to the right side of his body. He drooled too much to be a normally healthy child.

"The family doctor assured us that nothing was wrong, that he'd outgrow it. But we knew something was seriously wrong, so we took him to a specialist. Incredibly, the specialist diagnosed his condition as a version of club feet, and even treated him for that for several weeks.

"But we knew it was more serious than that. So we took him to yet another specialist. After extensive examination, the specialist said, 'This little boy is spastic. He has cerebral palsy. He's never going to be able to walk or talk or count to ten. I suggest that you put him in an institution for his own good and for the good of the normal members of the family.'"

When Bernie told me the story, he looked at me, and his dark eyes were flashing. He said, "But Zig, I'm not a buyer; I'm a seller. When this doctor said to me that I should consign my son to the life of a vegetable, I could not buy that idea, so I went to another doctor and another and yet another. Thirty different specialists in effect said, 'There is no hope for this little boy.'"

Then the Lofchicks heard of one more specialist, Dr. Perlstein, down in Chicago, at that time the foremost authority on cerebral palsy. Dr. Perlstein was booked over two years in advance with people from all over the world, but twelve days later, there was a cancellation, and they got an alternate appointment.

The family went down to Chicago, and Dr. Perlstein examined this little boy as no child has ever been examined before. He did a couple of things that were significantly different from what the other doctors had done. Each of them had simply taken the X-rays and the findings of the previous doctors, and all they did was agree with what the one before had said.

Dr. Perlstein started over. He took a brand-new set of X-rays. He called in the foremost authority on reading X-rays that was available and asked him to tell him what he saw. When he finished reading those X-rays, he went in to personally examine David. He told the Lofchicks, "This little boy is a spastic. He has cerebral palsy. He is never going to be able to walk or talk or count to ten, if you listen to the prophets of doom. But I want you to know that I am not problem-conscious, I am solution-conscious. I believe that if you are willing to do your part, there is in fact something that can be done for this little boy."

"Doctor, you name the price, and we'll pay it," said the Lofchicks. At that time, they could not easily afford a heavy financial burden.

The doctor spelled it out clearly: "You're going to have to push this little boy beyond all human endurance, and then you're going to have to push him some more. You're going to have to work him until he actually falls. Then you're going to have to work him some more.

"You've got to understand that once you have made your commitment, it is a forever commitment. If you ever stop, he will go back to where he was. You've got to understand that sometimes you're going to be working with him for months, maybe even years, before you can detect any progress. But if you stop it, again, he goes all the way back."

The doctor said one more thing: "You must never let him take therapy in the presence of other victims of cerebral palsy, because he will pick up their awkward, uncertain, unsure movements himself. You must not give him therapy with other victims."

The Lofchicks went home. They built a gymnasium down in the basement of their home. They hired a physical therapist and a bodybuilder, and they went to work. It took them several years, but finally one day little David Lofchick could move the limbs of his own body.

One day the therapist called Bernie and said, "I believe that David is ready. Why don't you come home and see?"

Bernie rushed home. David was down in the gymnasium on a mat, getting ready to do a push-up. As he started to rise into the air, the physical and emotional exertion was so great that there was not a dry inch of skin on that little body. The mat looked as if it had been sprinkled with water. Finally, when that one push-up was completed, mother and dad and David and the sisters and the neighbors, the therapist, the bodybuilder all broke down and shed tears. That clearly says that happiness is not pleasure; happiness is victory.

This story is even more remarkable when you understand that one of America's leading universities, which examined this little boy, said there was no motor connection to the right side of his body. "He has no sense of balance," they said. "He'll have extreme difficulty ever learning to walk. He'll never be able to swim or skate or ride a bicycle."

Finally, my wife and I had the privilege of flying to Winnipeg, to attend the bar mitzvah of little David Lofchick. I wish that you could have witnessed what we did: this little boy walking tall and straight and strong to the front of the synagogue, saying those words that moved him into the profession of faith of his forefathers. I wish you could have listened to him as he clearly and distinctly spoke those vows of his religious beliefs. I wish you could see this little boy, who was supposedly never going to be able to walk, talk, or count to ten. He ran the wheels off of three bicycles before he started driving his own automobile. He skated on the neighborhood hockey team, did as many as a thousand push-ups in a single day, ran as much as six miles nonstop, and became one of the outstanding table tennis players in Winnipeg. As a seventh grader, he did extraordinarily well in ninth-grade mathematics. He grew into a man of 195 pounds, with a barrel for a chest. He shoots golf in the high eighties. He qualified for an unrated, ordinary $100,000 life insurance policy, which is the first and only time, to the best of our knowledge, that this has happened to a victim of cerebral palsy.

I saw this boy many times over the years, and I've often wondered how much bigger, faster, stronger, and smarter he would have been if he had only had the privilege of having a normal birth and a normally healthy body. A few years later, it dawned on me that had this boy been given more, he might well have ended up with less, maybe a great deal less.

The story of David Lofchick says everything that I've tried to say throughout this book. David Lofchick did not start life with a healthy self-image, but he started working from a foundation that was extraordinarily solid. He had the advantage of having parents who not only loved him but saw him properly.

You see, you're going to treat people as you see them. They did not see David as a helpless, hopeless invalid. They looked at him as a baby and said, "Someday he is going to be a man, and he deserves his chance in life." You treat people as you see them, and they respond to the treatment. I'm convinced that that's why David was able to do so much.

Bernie Lofchick was in the world of sales and people development. Because of this, and because he understood completely that you can get everything in life that you want if you will just help enough other people get what they want, Bernie became a wealthy man. He had to work smarter, and he had to work harder. He had to develop other people who could carry on and do the same thing that he was doing.

Of all the families that I have ever seen in my life, there has never been one that has had more and bigger goals than the Lofchicks had for this little boy. They dreamed that their boy would have his chance in life. There were big goals, there were long-range goals, and there were daily goals. It was all put together in an attitude. Since this boy was about three years old, he listened to motivational audio recordings every day—as he was bathing, as he was taking therapy, as he was being taken to school. His whole attitude has been one of optimism and enthusiasm, and it's been pumped ten thousand times: *I can, I can, I can.*

I believe that man is designed for accomplishment. I believe he's engineered for success. I believe he's endowed with the seeds of greatness. We read in John 15:7: "If ye abide in me, and my words abide in you, ye shall ask what ye will, and it shall be done unto you." In other words, when we tie ourselves to the power of Almighty God, we remove all of the ceilings. We can go where we want to go, do what we want to do, be what we want to be.

Let me tell you about David Lofchick. For one solid winter with the wind chill hitting dozens of degrees below zero, David Lofchick would set his alarm clock one full hour earlier than any other member of the family. He would get up, strap his skates on his feet, and crawl out to the frozen swimming pool. He spent one solid winter just learning how to stand up.

Sometimes we get a little discouraged. Let me tell you about discouragement. A person may say, "I only have twenty-four hours out of every day." Let me tell you how many hours David Lofchick has had all of his life: twenty-one. He's got to spend three hours every day just staying even, because if he doesn't spend those three hours staying even, he's got to back up.

If you ask the Lofchicks, "Do you believe you've paid a price for good health?" I believe they will tell you with total certainty that there was no paying of a price. It was enjoying the price. When you look at David today, you know exactly what I'm talking about. We look at the stairway to the top, and we know a tremendous amount of desire was involved. It was an overwhelming desire that did not confuse pleasure with happiness.

Pleasure is what you enjoy for the moment. Yes, you might enjoy going bowling. Yes, you might get a little temporary pleasure out of goofing off for the evening. But I'm convinced that you enjoy happiness as a result of enjoying the price along the way.

There was a desire, and yes, the Lofchicks are privileged to live and work in a free enterprise system, just as you and I are. But let me also add one other ingredient that's obvious in this story, and that is the thing that we call love.

It's a different kind of love. It's the love that's so deep, so complete, and so total that it often says no. Many parents who lack a good self-image are afraid to say no to the whims of their children, for fear that the child will reject their love, but real love understand something much deeper.

Many nights, hundreds of nights, as the Lofchicks would start to put those braces on little David's legs as they put him to bed, with tears streaming down his cheeks he would say, "Can we leave them off just a night?" Or, "Can you leave them a little looser for just a night? Oh, please, mommy, don't tighten the braces tonight. Don't make me wear them."

If you are a parent, you fully know what I'm saying. How difficult it must have been to have resisted what he was requesting. But because they did say no to the tears of the moment, they were able to say yes to the laughter of a lifetime. I'm convinced that that's what love really is all about.

As we talk about what success is, what happiness is, what life is, I want to say that if you're going to climb that stairway, we also need to be aware of something else that's very significant. Again, I think it's wrapped up in a story.

A number of years ago, an old recluse lived on a hill above Venice, Italy. It was reputed that this old man could answer any question that anybody might ever ask. Two young boys determined to fool him. They caught a small bird, and they approached the old man with this question: "Is the bird alive or dead?" Without changing his expression, the old man said, "Son, if I say to you that the bird is alive, you will simply close your hands and crush him, and he'll be dead. If I say to you that the bird is dead, you'll simply open your hands and he'll fly away, because, you see, son, in your hands you hold the power of life and death."

I'll add that in your hands you hold the power of success or failure.

I'm going to close by giving you a choice. There are two trees that I want to talk about. One of them is a bonsai. It's raised by the Japanese. They have developed their techniques for growing this type of tree, and although it's perfect in proportion, it grows to the height of only eighteen to twenty-four inches.

In California, there is another tree: the sequoia named the General Sherman. This is a magnificent tree, extending to 275 feet into the heavens and 79 feet in circumference. This tree is so large that if you cut it down and sawed it up into lumber, it could build 35 five-room houses.

Now the General Sherman and the bonsai started at exactly the same size. Each weighed less than 1/3000 of an ounce. But the bonsai tree was removed from its roots. It was deliberately stunted in growth, so it grew only to a miniature size. On the other hand, the General Sherman grew in the rich soil of California. It was nourished by the minerals in that soil, fed by the rainfall, and nourished by the sunshine. It was permitted to grow into the giant that it eventually became.

You have a choice: you can grow into a giant, or you can remain a bonsai. I'm deeply persuaded that God wants you to be a giant. The choice is yours. What will it be, a General Sherman or a bonsai? I'm betting you're going to be a General Sherman.